JAMES RYDER RANDALL

(AT TWENTY-TWO)

WHEN MARYLAND, MY MARYLAND, WAS WRITTEN

# MARYLAND, MY MARYLAND
# AND OTHER POEMS

BY

## James Ryder Randall

JOHN MURPHY COMPANY
Publishers
BALTIMORE, MD. NEW YORK

TO THE MEMORY
OF
MY MOTHER

## CONTENTS

## POEMS OF JAMES RYDER RANDALL

## CONTENTS

# INTRODUCTION

These poems have been collected and are published at the request of the many friends of James Ryder Randall, who died on the 15th day of January, 1908, in Augusta, Ga.

Mr. Randall was born in Maryland, and, although circumstances compelled him to live for many years far away from his native State, he never lost his intense love for the place of his birth, and it was the hope of his life, in later years, to close his career in dear old Maryland.

When he was last in Baltimore, he was persuaded to surrender to friends the stray poems, which he had written, at various times, that they might be published in book form.

His great poem, which Oliver Wendell Holmes declared to be the greatest war song of any nation,

"Maryland, My Maryland," constitutes the main feature of this publication. The circumstances under which it was penned are thus described by himself:

"In April, 1861, I read in the New Orleans Delta news of the attack on the Massachusetts troops as they passed through Baltimore.

"This account greatly excited me. I had long been absent from my native city, and the startling event there influenced my mind. That night I could not dismiss from my mind what I had read in the paper. About midnight I arose, lit a candle and went to my desk. Some powerful influence seemed to possess me, and almost involuntarily I proceeded to write the song of 'My Maryland.'

"I remember that this idea seemed to take shape as music in my brain—some wild air that I can not now recall. The whole poem was dashed off rapidly when once begun. It was not composed in cold blood, but under what may be called a conflagration of the senses, if not an inspiration of the intellect. No one was more surprised than I was at the wide-spread and instantaneous popularity I had been so strangely stimulated to write."

# INTRODUCTION

Mr. Randall was, at the time, a Professor of English Literature and Classics in Poydras College at Pointe Coupee, Louisiana. While he was, thus, engaged, poetry was with him a passion and he had often, in the hours of leisure indulged in the ecstacy of writing exquisite poetry.

Published in the last days of April, 1861, his war song fired the Southern heart.

It displays the warmth of youth with the valor of the soldier, and pleads with his mother State to vindicate her peerless chivalry. After the war, his deep religious devotion turned his heart in kindness to those, who had been on the other side in the fratricidal strife, and he wrote the beautiful poem "At Arlington." A devoted friend of Colonel Randall thus described the circumstances under which that poem was written. In the hearts of some of his triumphant foes the gall of bitterness still lingered, and "on one Decoration Day," so the story goes, "the graves of Federal soldiers at Arlington Cemetery were heaped with flowers, and some pious women strewed a few garlands on the nearby graves of some Confederate dead. Whereupon, some Northern men, who saw the loving act, trampled under foot the garlands placed on the "Rebel Sod."

But when the sun rose next morning the flowers were decking the Confederate graves and this was how it happened:

Jehovah judged, abashing man:
  For in the vigils of the night,
His mighty storm-avengers ran
  Together in one choral clan,
Rebuking wrong, rewarding right;
  Plucking the wreaths from those who won,
The tempest, heaped them dewy bright
  On Rebel graves at Arlington.

Other poems of rare beauty adorn this little book; but the grandest of all in spirituality of thought, in sublime religious faith and in beseeching supplication is that of "Resurgam:"

Banished from thee! where shall I find
  For my poor soul
A safe retreat from storms that blind
  Or seas that roll?
Come to me, Christ, ere I forlorn,
  Sink 'neath the wave,
And on this blessed Easter morn
  A lost one, save!

## INTRODUCTION

This collection of poems is, now, sent forth in the hope of the author's friends, that it may receive a large share of favor from the public for the benefit of the family of the deceased author and poet, James Ryder Randall.

*Baltimore, February* 7, 1908.

*Oliver Wendell Holmes once said of Maryland, My Maryland: "My only regret is that I could not do for Massachusetts what Randall did for Maryland."*

## MARYLAND, MY MARYLAND

The despot's heel is on thy shore,
Maryland!
His touch is at thy temple door,
Maryland!
Avenge the patriotic gore
That flecked the streets of Baltimore,
And be the battle queen of yore,
Maryland! My Maryland!

Hark to a wand'ring son's appeal,
Maryland!
My mother State! to thee I kneel,
Maryland!
For life and death, for woe and weal,
Thy peerless chivalry reveal,
And gird thy beauteous limbs with steel,
Maryland! My Maryland!

Thou wilt not cower in the dust,
Maryland!
Thy beaming sword shall never rust,
Maryland!
Remember Carroll's sacred trust,
Remember Howard's warlike thrust,—
And all thy slumberers with the just,
Maryland! My Maryland!

Come! 'tis the red dawn of the day,
Maryland!
Come with thy panoplied array,
Maryland!
With Ringgold's spirit for the fray,
With Watson's blood at Monterey,
With fearless Lowe and dashing May,
Maryland! My Maryland!

Come! for thy shield is bright and strong,
Maryland!
Come! for thy dalliance does thee wrong,
Maryland!
Come to thine own heroic throng,
That stalks with liberty along,
And gives a new *Key* to thy song,
Maryland! My Maryland!

## MARYLAND, MY MARYLAND

Dear Mother! burst the tyrant's chain,
        Maryland!
Virginia should not call in vain,
        Maryland!
She meets her sisters on the plain—
*"Sic semper!"* 'tis the proud refrain
That baffles minions back again,
        Maryland! My Maryland!

I see the blush upon thy cheek,
        Maryland!
But thou wast ever bravely meek,
        Maryland!
But lo! there surges forth a shriek
From hill to hill, from creek to creek—
Potomac calls to Chesapeake,
        Maryland! My Maryland!

Thou wilt not yield the Vandal toll,
        Maryland!
Thou wilt not crook to his control,
        Maryland!
Better the fire upon thee roll,
Better the blade, the shot, the bowl,
Than crucifixion of the soul,
        Maryland! My Maryland!

I hear the distant thunder hum,
Maryland!
The Old Line's bugle, fife, and drum,
Maryland!
She is not dead, nor deaf, nor dumb—
Huzza! she spurns the Northern scum!
She breathes! she burns! she'll come! she'll come!
Maryland! My Maryland!

---

## PELHAM

Just as the Spring came laughing through the strife,
With all its gorgeous cheer;
In the bright April of historic life,
Fell the great cannoneer.

A wondrous lulling of a hero's breath,
His bleeding country weeps;
Hushed in the alabaster arms of Death,
Our young Marcellus sleeps.

Nobler and grander than the Child of Rome,
Curbing his chariot steeds;
The knightly scion of a Southern home,
Dazzled the land with deeds.

## PELHAM

Gentlest and bravest in the battle's brunt,
  The Champion of the Truth;
He won his banner in the very front
  Of our immortal youth.

A clang of sabres 'mid Virginian snow,
  The fiery pang of shells—
And there's a wail of immemorial woe
  In Alabama dells.

The pennon droops that led the sacred band
  Along the crimson field;
The meteor blade sinks from the nerveless hand
  Over the spotless shield.

We gazed and gazed upon that beauteous face,
  While 'round the lips and eyes,
Couched in their marble slumber, flashed the grace
  Of a divine surprise.

O Mother of a blessed soul on high!
  Thy tears may soon be shed—
Think of thy boy with princes of the sky,
  Among the Southern Dead.

How must he smile on this dull world beneath,
  Favored with swift renown;
He with the martyr's amaranthine wreath
  Twining the victor's crown!

## THERE'S LIFE IN THE OLD LAND YET*

By blue Patapsco's billowy dash
  The Tyrant's war shout comes,
Along with the cymbal's fitful clash
  And the growl of his sullen drums;
We hear it—we heed it, with vengeful thrills,
  And we shall not forgive or forget—
There's faith in the streams, there's hope in the hills,
  There's Life in the Old Land yet!

Minions! we sleep, but we are not dead,
  We are crushed—we are scourged—we are scarred—
We crouch—'tis to welcome the triumph-tread
  Of the peerless Beauregard.
Then woe to your vile, polluting horde
  When the Southern braves are met—
There's faith in the victor's stainless sword—
  There's Life in the Old Land yet!

*Not to be confused with the song by A. F. Gibson, and dedicated to Severn Teackle Wallis. This poem by Mr. Randall was set to music under the title, "We Sleep, but We are Not Dead."

## THERE'S LIFE IN THE OLD LAND YET

Bigots! ye quell not the valiant mind
With the clank of an iron chain;
The Spirit of Freedom sings in the wind
O'er Merryman, Thomas, and Kane!
And we—though we smite not—are not thralls,
We are piling a gory debt;
While down by McHenry's dungeon walls
There's Life in the Old Land yet!

Our women have hung their harps away,
And they scowl on your brutal bands,
While the nimble poniard dares the day
In their dear, defiant hands!
They will strip their tresses to string our bows
Ere the Northern sun is set—
There's faith in their unrelenting woes,
There's Life in the Old Land yet!

There's life, though it throbbeth in silent veins,
'Tis vocal without noise—
It gushed o'er Manassas' solemn plains
*From the blood of the Maryland boys!*
That blood shall cry aloud, and rise
With an everlasting threat—
By the death of the brave, by the God in the skies,
There's Life in the Old Land yet!

## JOHN W. MORTON

Ringed with flame and sore beset,
Where gunboat and rifle fire met;
Where cannon blazed from water and land
Upon the Donelson Southern band,
A gallant lad of nineteen years,
A stranger to tremor and to fears,
Stood by a battery piece and shot
The first shell in that crater hot.

His captain, Porter, smitten down
Where all the volleyed thunders frown,
Shouted, when borne in pain away:
"John, don't give up that gun, I say!
"No! not while a man is left," replied
The lad, in the flush of martial pride;
And he kept his word to the utter end,
While a man could live in that river bend.

## JOHN W. MORTON

"No prison for me", grim Forrest said,
And thousands followed where he led.
But other thousands remained because
They bowed to Buckner's word and laws.
Whelmed by the girdling Northern men,
They marched to the captive's dismal den,
And the lad who fired the first gun past
Into that solitude sad and vast.

A few months more, and the daring boy
Breathed the air that the free enjoy.
A few months more, and he gayly went
Where dauntless Forrest pitched his tent.
Saluting the hero, he quickly gave
To the South's own "bravest of the brave"
A paper that said he was to be
The Wizard's Chief of Artillery.

A derisive smile swept over the face
Of the stern commander, in his place.
"What!" he growled, "are you to wield
Command of my guns in war's fierce field?
Nonsense, boy, go grow a beard!"
And this was what the stripling heard.

But presently the Wizard's brow
Grew calm. "I'll try you, anyhow",
He said, and from that setting sun
Morton and Forrest were as one.

Nigh four tremendous, bloody years,
Full of combat, smiles and tears;
O'er miles of land in battles grand,
Forrest and Morton went hand in hand.
With sword and pistol the Wizard slew,
While Morton's guns mowed men in blue.
If mortal man could ever have freed
The South from the foeman's grasp and greed,
That man was Forrest, but we see
It was not destined so to be.

II.

Long years have gone, the grass is spread
Above the bivouacs of the dead.
The mighty Wizard's wand is still
Like his heart; but from every Southern hill,
And mount and stream and vale bedight,
With sun and moon and star alight,
He lives in glorious deeds, alway,
Baffling the onset of decay.

## JOHN W. MORTON

The lad who made the cannon roar
Survives on Life's tumultuous shore.
His locks are silvered, but his brain
Burns with heroic throbs amain.
Gentle and kind, but valiant yet,
Forgiving, he cannot forget
The Cause he fought for, with his mate
Immortal, whatsoe'er its fate;
While from his great dark eyes there gleams
The orient of remembered dreams.

And now the old bard's final rhyme
Invokes a blessing of Easter time,
Upon his people and home and race,
Like manna-dew of heavenly grace.
With higher aims, in war's surcease,
Be thou allied with the Prince of Peace,
And never, henceforth, forget to be
"Soldier of Him who died for thee."

## ON THE RAMPART

On Sumter's rampart, that sweet eve,
  I heard the vesper bugle play
In chorus with the ocean's heave,
  All in the golden prime of May.

On either side, the level lands
  Swam seaward gray and serpentine;
The billows burst in corsair bands
  Against their shield of rock and pine.

Aloof, beyond the sullen bar
  Crouching, the black armada rides—
Afront the vulture ships of war,
  Brooded the giant Ironsides.

The fortress guns scowled from their lair
  Along the sentry's bristling beat;
While on the sultry wave, aglare,
  Back frowned the gaunt and baffled fleet.

## ON THE RAMPART

Above her, in the glittering day,
  The white-winged banner's battle stars.
Crisping the bosom of the bay,
  Bold Moultrie stands with all her scars;

Amid the island, in repose,
  The casual breeze at last grew still;
And, through the haze of twilight, rose
  The tower of Secessionville.

The patient moon clomb up the sky
  Forever on the sun god's trail—
The saddest, loveliest thing on high,
  And like Oenone's passion pale.

The signal fires wink through the dark
  Aleft and right, as rays may reach
Around the red and feverish arc
  Of muffled batteries on the beach.

A hallowed radiance, calm and grave,
  Gilded the city's storied spires,
Where watch the beautiful and brave,
  Where sleep the Carolinian sires.

On Sumter's rampart, that sweet night,
  Leaning beside the shattered wall,
Thy gentle face, so fair and bright,
  Kept me, dear love, within thy thrall.

I turned from wrecks of storm and strife
  To thee— within some distant home;
I felt that all my fate and life
  Were thine, wherever I must roam.

A glory has come o'er my days
  In dreaming noblest dreams of thee;
Beyond the rampart, how my gaze
  Went proudly o'er the Southern sea!

And dreams like mine can still defy
  Even the tempest of distrust;
I know that they shall never die
  Because they are not of the dust.

Dear love! though dreams may wither here,
  They are upgathered from the sod,
And we shall see them reappear
  In the long summer time of God!

•

## MEMORIAL DAY

Noblest of martyrs in a glorious fight!
Ye died to save the cause of Truth and Right.
And though your banner beams no more on high,
Not vainly did it wave or did ye die!

No blood for freedom shed is spent in vain;
It is as fertile as the Summer rain;
And the last tribute of heroic breath
Is always conqueror over Wrong and Death.

The grand procession of avenging years
Has turned to triumph all our bitter tears;
And the cause lost, by battle's stern behest,
Is won by Justice, and by Heaven blest.

Dark grew the night above our sacred slain,
Who sleeps upon the mountain and the plain;
But darker still the black and blinding pall
That whelmed the living in its lurid thrall.

But taught by heroes, who had yielded life,
We fainted not, nor faltered in the strife;
With weapons bright, from peaceful Reason won,
We cleaved the clouds and gained the golden sun.

And so today the marble shaft may soar
In memory of those who are no more;
The proudest boast of centuries shall be,
That they who fell with JACKSON rise with LEE!

---

## THE BATTLE CRY OF THE SOUTH

Arm yourselves and be valiant men, and see that we be in readiness against the morning, that ye may fight with these nations that are assembled against us, to destroy us and our sanctuary.

For it is better for us to die in battle than to behold the calamities of our people and our sanctuary.—Maccabees 1.

Brothers! the thunder-cloud is black,
And the wail of the South wings forth;
Will ye cringe to the hot tornado's rack,
And the Vampires of the North?
Strike! ye can win a martyr's goal;
Strike! with a ruthless hand—
Strike! with the vengeance of the soul
For your bright, beleaguered land!
To arms! to arms! for the South needs help,
And a craven is he who flees—
For ye have the sword of the Lion's Whelp,*
And the God of the Maccabees!

*The surname of the great Maccabees.

## THE BATTLE CRY OF THE SOUTH

Arise! though the stars have a rugged glare,
  And the moon has a wrath-blurred crown—
Brothers! a blessing is ambushed there
  In the cliffs of the Father's frown;
Arise! ye are worthy the wondrous light
  Which the Sun of Justice gives—
In the caves and sepulchres of night
  Jehovah the Lord King lives!
    To arms! to arms! for the South needs help,
      And a craven is he who flees—
    For ye have the sword of the Lion's Whelp,
      And the God of the Maccabees!

Think of the dead by the Tennessee
  In their frozen shrouds of gore—
Think of the mothers who shall see
  Those darling eyes no more!
But better are they in a hero-grave
  Than the serfs of time and breath,
For they are the Children of the Brave,
  And the Cherubim of Death!
    To arms! to arms! for the South needs help,
      And a craven is he who flees—
    For ye have the sword of the Lion's Whelp,
      And the God of the Maccabees!

Better the charnels of the West
  And a hecatomb of lives,
Than the foul invader as a guest,
  'Mid your sisters and your wives—
But a spirit lurketh in every maid,
  Though, brothers, ye should quail,
To sharpen a Judith's lurid blade,
  And the livid spike of Jael!
    To arms! to arms! for the South needs help,
      And a craven is he who flees—
    For ye have the sword of the Lion's Whelp,
      And the God of the Maccabees!

Brothers! I see you tramping by,
  With the gladiator gaze,
And your shout is the Macedonian cry
  Of old, heroic days!
March on! with trumpet and with drum,
  With rifle, pike, and dart,
And die—if even death must come—
  Upon your country's heart.
    To arms! to arms! for the South needs help,
      And a craven is he who flees—
    For ye have the sword of the Lion's Whelp,
      And the God of the Maccabees!

## THE BATTLE CRY OF THE SOUTH

Brothers! the thunder cloud is black,
  And the wail of the South wings forth;
Will ye cringe to the hot tornado's rack,
  And the Vampires of the North?
Strike! ye can win a martyr's goal,
  Strike! with a ruthless hand;
Strike! with the vengeance of the soul
  For your bright, beleaguered land!
    To arms! to arms! for the South needs help,
      And a craven is he who flees—
    For ye have the sword of the Lion's whelp,
      And the God of the Maccabees!

## THE LONE SENTRY

Previous to the first battle of Manassas, when the troops under Stonewall Jackson had made a forced march, on halting at night they fell on the ground, exhausted and faint. The hour arrived for setting the watch for the night. The officer of the day went to the General's tent and said:

"General, the men are all wearied and there is not one but is asleep. Shall I wake them?"

"No," said the noble Jackson. "Let them sleep, and I will watch the camp tonight."

And all night long he rode around that lonely camp, the one lone sentinel for that brave, but weary, body of Virginia heroes. When glorious morning broke, the soldiers awoke fresh and ready for action, all unconscious of the vigil kept over their slumbers.

'Twas at the dying of the day,
The darkness grew so still
The drowsy pipe of evening birds
Was hushed upon the hill.
Athwart the shadows of the vale
Slumbered the men of might,
And one lone sentry paced his rounds
To watch the camp that night.

## THE LONE SENTRY

A grave and solemn man was he,
  With deep and somber brow;
The dreamful eyes seemed hoarding up
  Some unaccomplished vow.
The wistful glance peered o'er the plain
  Beneath the starry light,
And with the murmured name of God
  He watched the camp that night.

The future opened unto him
  Its grand and awful scroll—
Manassas and the Valley march
  Came heaving o'er his soul,
Richmond and Sharpsburg thundered by
  With that tremendous fight
That gave him to the angel host
  Who watched the camp that night.

We mourn for him who died for us
  With one resistless moan,
While up the Valley of the Lord
  He marches to the Throne!
He kept the faith of men and saints
  Sublime and pure and bright;
He sleeps—and all is well with him
  Who watched the camp that night.

Brothers! The midnight of our Cause
  Is shrouded in our fate—
The demon Goths pollute our halls
  With fire and lust and hate!
Be strong, be valiant, be assured—
  Strike home for Heaven and Right!
The soul of Jackson stalks abroad
  And guards the camp tonight.

---

## AT FORT PILLOW

You shudder as you think upon
  The carnage of the grim report,
The desolation when we won
  The inner trenches of the fort.

But there are deeds you may not know
  That scourge the pulses into strife;
Dark memories of deathless woe
  Pointing the bayonet and knife.

## AT FORT PILLOW

The house is ashes where I dwelt
  Beyond the mighty inland sea,
The tombstones shattered where I knelt
  By that old church upon the lee.

The prowling fiends who came with fire
  Camped on the consecrated sod,
And trampled in the dust and mire
  The holy tenement of God!

The spot where darling mother sleeps,
  Beneath the glimpse of yon sad moon,
Is crushed, with splintered marble heaps,
  To stall the horse of some dragoon.

And when I ponder that black day,
  It makes my frantic spirit wince;
I marched—with Longstreet—far away,
  But have beheld the ravage since.

The tears are hot upon my face,
  When thinking what bleak fate befell
  The only sister of our race—
  A thing too horrible to tell.

They say that ere her senses fled,
  She rescued, of her brothers cried,
Then feebly bowed her stricken head,
  Too good to live thus—so she died.

Two of those brothers heard no plea,
With their proud hearts for ever still—
Guy, shrouded by the Tennessee,
And Bertram at the Malvern Hill.

But I have heard it everywhere,
Vibrating like a mystic knell;
'Tis as perpetual as the air
And solemn as a funeral bell.

By scorched lagoon and murky swamp,
My wrath was never in the lurch;
I've killed the picket in his camp,
And many a pilot on his perch.

With steady rifle, sharpened brand,
A week ago, upon my steed,
With Forrest and his warrior band,
I made the hell-hounds writhe and bleed.

You should have seen our leader go
Upon the battle's burning marge,
Swooping, like falcon, on the foe,
Heading the gray line's iron charge.

All outcasts from our ruined marts,
We heard th' undying serpent hiss,
And, in the desert of our hearts,
The fatal spell of Nemesis.

## AT FORT PILLOW

The Southern yell rang loud and high,
  The moment that we thundered in,
Smiting the demons hip and thigh,
  Cleaving them to the very chin.

My right arm, bared for fiercer play,
  The left one held the rein in slack;
In all the fury of the fray,
  I sought the white man, not the black.

The dabbled clots of brain and gore
  Across the swirling sabers ran;
To me each brutal visage bore
  The front of one accursed man.

Trobbing along the frenzied vein,
  My blood seemed kindled into song—
The death-dirge of the sacred slain,
  The slogan of immortal wrong.

It glared athwart the dripping glaives—
  It blazed in each avenging eye—
*The thought of desecrated graves*
  *And some lone sister's desperate cry!*

*Wilmington, April* 25, 1864.

## OUR CONFEDERATE DEAD

Unknown to me, brave boy, but still I wreathe
  For you the tenderest of wildwood flowers;
And o'er your tomb a virgin's prayer I breathe
  To greet the pure moon and the April showers.

I only know, I only care to know,
  You died for me—for me and country bled;
A thousand Springs and wild December snow
  Will weep for one of all the Southern Dead.

Perchance some mother gazes up the skies,
  Wailing, like Rachel, for her martyred brave—
Oh, for her darling sake, my dewy eyes
  Moisten the turf above your lowly grave.

The cause is sacred, when our maidens stand
  Linked with sad matrons and heroic sires,
Above the relics of a vanquished land,
  And light the torch of sanctifying fires.

## OUR CONFEDERATE DEAD

Your bed of honor has a rosy cope,
  To shimmer back the tributary stars;
And every petal glistens with a hope
  When Love has blossomed in the disk of Mars.

Sleep! On your couch of glory slumber comes
  Bosomed amid th' archangelic choir,
Not with the grumble of impetuous drum,
  Deep'ning the chorus of embattled ire.

Above you shall the oak and cedar fling
  Their giant plumage and protecting shade;
For you the song-bird pause upon its wing
  And warble requiem ever undismayed.

Farewell! And, if your spirit wander near
  To kiss this plaint of unaspiring art—
Translated, even in the heavenly sphere,
  As the libretto of a maiden's heart.

## PLACIDE BOSSIER

Ah, friend! in the tender College time
  No evil deed could stain thee,
And now 'mid the combat's iron chime,
  In purity they've slain thee.
Sans peur et sans reproche to live,
  Sans peur the foe defying—
Sans peur et sans reproche we give
  Thy epitaph when dying.

When the Southern bullet sang the knell
  Of the butchering invader,
Then—then triumphantly he fell,
  Our spotless young Crusader;
With the loud hurrah and the dauntless tramp
  Of the charging Creole yoemen,
He fell where the Cherubim encamp,
  With his face to the flying foemen.

The blood moon guides its torch of night
  Through the smoke envolumed valleys,
And the hillocks tell where the reddest fight
  Shook the quick, convulsive vollies;
In the foremost phalanx he shall rest
  His head in the dust declining,
The rifle shielding the soldier breast—
  The cross on the saint-heart shining!

## ASHES

The Spring will come with its ebullient blood,
  With flush of roses and imperial eyes;
A vein of strength will throb along the flood—
Banners of beauty toss the pillared wood
  When birds of music anthem to the skies.

And man prowls forth to mar thy gentle ways,
  With sword and shot and sacrilegious hand;
Thy reign is fallen upon demon days,
We peer at thee althrough a gory haze,
  Weeping and praying for our stricken land.

O Land! O Land! of benignant South!
  The Great High Priest approaches to thy brow,
Anointing it with ashes; let thy mouth
Rebel not, nor thy heart be filled with drouth—
  The hand will raise thee up that smites thee now.

*Ash Wednesday,* 1865.

# POEMS OF JAMES RYDER RANDALL

## THE UNCONQUERED BANNER

"A Lost Cause!" If lost, it was false; if true, it is not lost. If the Cause is lost, the Constitution is lost; the Union, defined by it is lost; the liberty of the States and the people, which they both at first and for half a century guarded, are lost."—Henry A. Wise.

"Yet, Freedom yet, thy banner, torn though flying,
Streams, like a thunderstorm, against the wind."
—Byron.

The sad priest-singer, in his dread despair,
When our war-trumpets ceased their charging blare,
Wailed, in melodious numbers, o'er the South,
Her righteous Cause crushed at the cannon-mouth.
He bade us fold our banner and for aye,
Because its night had come and not one ray
Of hope remained to gild its glorious head,
And that it typified the hopeless dead.

## THE UNCONQUERED BANNER

The peerless poet of that desperate age
Wrote an immortal lyric, but the rage
Of the aggressive section is no more,
And thus our Southern flag, from shore to shore,
Emerges like an eagle from its sleep
To woo the sun, and, in its heart to keep
The never-dying principle of Right,
Surviving every fierce, unequal fight.

Men die, but principles can know no death—
No last extinguishment of mortal breath.
We fought for what our fathers held in trust;
It did not fall forever in the dust.
Our foemen sought to make us worse than slaves
And envy all who sleep in hero-graves;
They failed at last to do the deed they meant—
They failed in trying God to circumvent.

And well for them they failed, for, in the end,
Their fate and ours must ever interblend,
If we have Cæsar, so must Cæsar be
With them in fullest perpetuity.
If they have empire and the sordid ban
Of Shylock and the money-changing clan;
The South is blameless; for she holds in fee
The stainless swords of Washington and Lee.

There was scant glory in our overthrow—
Not Valor did it, but a brutal blow.
Five hundred thousand Hessians and a horde
Of blacks and Tories broke the Southern Sword.
Shut from the sea, o'erwhelmed upon the land,
We fought the battle to a final stand.
But the Great Cause, outlasting all debates,
Lives in free union of unfettered States.

Now, let our Banner, symbol of the Right,
Kiss every wind in its unconquered might;
Let the glad spirit of the poet-priest
Hover above this grand Reunion feast
To watch our Banner, from the grave of strife
Rise with the glory of a new-born life;
Twined with the ancient flag, o'er land and main,
And wed to deathless liberty again.

# AT ARLINGTON

## AT ARLINGTON

On the day that the graves of the Federal soldiers buried at Arlington were decorated, in 1869, a number of ladies entered the cemetery for the purpose of placing flowers on the graves of thirty Confederates. Their progress was stopped by bayonets, and they were not allowed to perform their mission of love. During the night a high wind arose, and in the morning all the floral offerings that had been placed the day before upon the Federal graves were found piled upon the mounds under which reposed the thirty Confederates.

The broken column, reared in air
  To him who made our country great,
Can almost cast its shadow where
The victims of a grand despair,
  In long, long ranks of death await
    The last loud trump, the Judgment-Sun,
  Which come for all, and, soon or late,
    Will come for those at Arlington.

In that vast sepulchre repose
The thousands reaped from every fray;
The Men in Blue who once uprose
In battle-front to smite their foes—
The Spartan Bands who wore the grey;
The combat o'er, the death-hug done,
In summer blaze or winter snows,
They keep the truce at Arlington.

And almost lost in myriad graves,
Of those who gained the unequal fight,
Are mounds that hide Confederate braves,
Who reck not how the North wind raves,
In dazzling day or dimmest night,
O'er those who lost and those who won;
Death holds no parley which was right—
Jehovah judges Arlington.

The dead had rest; the Dove of Peace
Brooded o'er both with equal wings;
To both had come that great surcease,
The last omnipotent release
From all the world's delirious stings.
To bugle deaf and signal-gun,
They slept, like heroes of old Greece,
Beneath the glebe at Arlington.

## AT ARLINGTON

And in the Spring's benignant reign,
  The sweet May woke her harp of pines;
Teaching her choir a thrilling strain
Of jubilee to land and main,
  She danced in emerald down the lines.
    Denying largesse bright to none,
  She saw no difference in the signs
    That told who slept at Arlington.

She gave her grasses and her showers
  To all alike who dreamed in dust;
Her song-birds wove their dainty bowers
Amid the jasmine buds and flowers,
  And piped with an impartial trust;
    Waifs of the air and liberal sun,
  Their guileless glees were kind and just
    To friend and foe at Arlington.

And 'mid the generous spring there came
  Some women of the land, who strove
To make this funeral-field of fame
Glad as the May-God's altar flame,
  With rosy wreaths of mutual love—
    Unmindful who had lost or won,
They scorned the jargon of a name—
    No North, no South, at Arlington.

Between their pious thought and God
Stood files of men with brutal steel;
The garlands placed on "Rebel sod"
Were trampled in the common clod,
To die beneath the hireling heel.
Facing this triumph of the Hun,
Our Smoky Cæsar gave no nod,
To keep the peace at Arlington.

Jehovah judged—abashing man—
For in the vigils of the night,
His mighty storm-avengers ran
Together in one choral clan,
Rebuking wrong, rewarding right;
Plucking the wreaths from those who won.
The tempest heaped them dewy-bright
On REBEL graves at Arlington.

And when the morn came young and fair,
Brimful of blushes ripe and red,
Knee-deep in sky-sent roses there,
Nature began her earliest prayer
Above triumphant Southern dead.
So, in the dark and in the sun,
Our Cause survives the Tyrant's tread,
And sleeps to wake at Arlington.

# POEMS

## SENTIMENTAL AND MISCELLANEOUS

## PART SECOND

Beginning with "The Oriel Window", ending with "Resurgam"

# THE ORIEL WINDOW

## THE ORIEL WINDOW

I pray in the country church, alas!<br>
  With missal and mind contrary;<br>
And in spite of the hymn and the blessed Mass,<br>
  In spite of my Ave Mary,<br>
My fancies are drowned in the faces around,<br>
  In spite of my Ave Mary!

The bluffs, the breeze, the bulwark trees,<br>
  Are grand and glad and holy yet;<br>
The river as proudly seeks the seas<br>
  As it did in the days of Joilet—<br>
It's wave-lips stirr'd with the babble of a bird<br>
  As a psalm and a psalter for Joilet.

And then uprolled from the rafter's mold,
  Come the dear ones, the departed—
The fair and old 'neath the marigold,
  The bold and the broken-hearted—
Till I shudder to think how we rabble on the brink
  Of the early broken-hearted.

In mystic trance of my old Romance,
  I let all my sorrow and sin go;
Forgetting the graves as they glance and dance
  Down—down through the ghastly window—
With column and cross and banners of moss,
  Down—down through the Oriel Window.

A purple band from the Phantom Land,
  Come the idol-gods I cherished,
And lo! they stand by a throne of sand,
    With palsied brows and perished—
And scoop from the shore of the sea no more
  The shells of the Past and Perished.

But from those shells ring passion bells,
  Till my soul from its sacred duty
Is ravished along with an earthly song,
  But a song of love and beauty,
Till the air is aglow with lustrous hair
  And dark-eyed songs of beauty.

## THE ORIEL WINDOW

*She* kneels in a nook by the dusty choir,
  With aspect lost and lornful;
My breast is gored with spears of fire
  To see her looking so mournful—
Ah, 'tis not meet that one so sweet
  Should ever be moody and mournful.

She tells, I wist, the beads on her wrist,
  With a gentle, lyrical motion;
And she seems in a mist when the Eucharist
  Is soared for the people's devotion;
While a glittering crown for the head bowed down
  Is the meed of her dear devotion.

Have you come in the guise of Paradise
  Our heart-troth to dissever?
In tears, for the lonesome, bitter years,
  Would you woo me back forever?
Oh, speak, love, speak what your sad eyes seek,
  And win me back forever!

Both overthrown, we both have known
  How the chains of mortality clank ill—
But tonight, tonight a vow we'll plight,
  To make our wild hearts tranquil;
While the flambeaux shine over thine and mine
  Untroubled, untortured and tranquil.

* * * * * * * * *

*She* kneels in a nook by the dusty choir,
  Shakes the bloom from my dream-mimosa,
I rush to the nook in the choir to greet
  The Mater Dolorosa!
Nought, nought was there but a sculptured prayer
  Of the Mater Dolorosa.

No more in a trance of my old Romance
  Shall I let all my sorrow and sin go;
But I'll join the graves as they glance and dance
  Down—down through the ghastly window,
With column and cross, and banners of moss
  Down—down through the Oriel Window!

*Point Coupee on the Mississippi,* 1861.

## ANIMA

## ANIMA

You came to me in feeble health, the hectic on your
cheek,
Revealed to my adoring sight a body frail and weak;
The lissome form, the glamoured eyes, the spirit undefiled,
These, and a glimpse of early death, I saw, beloved
child!
And if, my guilty heart could dare to make your
heart its goal—
I did not love you for your face—I loved you for
your soul!

You came to me a waif of God, unsullied by deceit;
I felt it sacrilege to kiss the shadows of your feet.
And when your thoughts were magnified beyond the
dull terrene,
Me dreamt you sat within the Heaven beside the
Nazarene.
And if my fierce emotions seared your being like a
scroll—
I did not love you for your face—I love you for your
soul!

You came to me like manna dews—like an embodied prayer;
Till your imploring accents turned the torrent of despair.
You made me feel the blight of Sin, the majesty of Love,
And when I clutched an earthly crown, you merely glanced above.
Oh, gladly for you would these hands demand the beggar's dole—
I did not love you for your face—I loved you for your soul!

You left me, darling child, before the Promised Land was won,
And it was hard for me to look upon the living sun.
'Twas no ignoble whim that hoped to make you mine alway;
My idol was no frenzy of the perishable clay.
And if I kneel to you no more, save by the churchyard knoll,
I have not loved you for your face—I've loved you for your soul!

## EIDOLON

Ah, sweet-eyed Christ! Thy image smiles
  In its Cathedral cell,
Shrined in the heaven-enamored arms
  Of her who never fell;
And if my phantom eyes implore
  A more benignant beam,
'Tis a nepenthe I would crave
  For a memorial dream!

Dear Leonie! here did'st thou kneel
  That musky summer noon,
As the zephyrs kissed in ecstasy
  The dimpled cheeks of June—
As the sunlight drifted o'er thy brow
  A golden wave of grace,
Bright blending with the miracles
  Of that angelic face.

Adorably Madonna-like,
  By this communion rail,
Thy raptured face, though rich with youth,
  Was spirit-lit and pale;
And oh those opulent blue eyes,
  Those Meccas of despair—
They, they were glorious Eden-isles
  Lost in a lake of prayer!

Saint Leonie! I saw thee flit
  Gazelle-like to the street,
And pure, melodious angels led
  Thy dainty, tinkling feet;
My rebel thoughts were petrel-winged,
  Attendant upon thee,
Chasing thy loved and lissome shape
  As Arabs of the sea.

Long did I love thee, *belle Creole,*
  As Gebirs love the sun,
And in the temple of my soul
  Thou wast the eidolon;
Long did I love thee, *belle Creole,*
  Where corsair billows rise,
And where the silver planets soar
  In unfamiliar skies!

## EIDOLON

Dark Corcovado! did I not,
  With heart and soul aflame,
Carve on thy broad, monarchal brow
  Her wildly-worshipped name —
Watching the homeward ships scud by
  Before the nimble breeze,
Till memory with them wept away
  Beyond the tropic seas!

Years, years had died, and once again
  I saw the spires of home;
Then, armed with an undying hope,
  I stood beneath this dome.
But not within the pillared aisle,
  Nor by the sacred sign,
Could my bewildered eyes behold
  The loveliness of thine.

The sad November days had come,
  And eagerly I fled
To find thee where the maidens deck
  The kingdoms of the dead;
I found thee—yes, I found thee, love,
  Beneath the willow tree—
With marble cross and immortelle
  And one word—"Leonie!"

## THE DAMSEL OF MOBILE

I met thee in the Summer time,
  The Summer of my youth—
In days of my melodious prime
  And thine unsullied truth.
I met thee when the jasmine buds,
  Their velvet locks reveal;
'Til I loved thee, 'til I loved thee,
  Darling Damsel of Mobile!

O shining tresses of the sun!
  O eyes of ocean blue!
O dainty feet to nimbly run
  Upon the glittering dew!
The cypress breathes its gloomy buds
  On all I felt and feel—
Still I love thee! Still I love thee!
  Darling Damsel of Mobile!

## THE DAMSEL OF MOBILE

And now the Summer time no more,
  The vikings of the rain
Thunder their turf-steeds on the shore
  And prowl the jasmine plain;
The night shade blackens on my brow,
  The lightnings gash like steel—
But a Summer heart still throbs for thee,
  Darling Damsel of Mobile!

I know, I know that Summer goes,
  Like some divine disguise;
I know that Summer rapture flows
  By ringlets and blue eyes—
But thou, my Psyche and my soul!
  To thee alone I kneel,
With the Summer sunshine in thy hair,
  Darling Damsel of Mobile!

## THE DYING GIRL

Written at the Age of Sixteen

Earth is fading—heaven beaming—
  All around grows dark and chill;
White robed phantoms near me streaming—
  Streaming, streaming, streaming still.

Clasp me, mother, clasp me lightly,
  Lest you press the soul too soon
From the form that once shone brightly—
  Quenched its brilliance in its noon.

Kiss me, father, kiss me sweetly;
  Smoothe the ringlets from my brow—
Quick—oh quick—for fleetly, fleetly
  Speeds life's current from me now!

Where is Harry, where is Harry?
  Far from Stella's weeping bed;
Who to him my words shall carry—
  Who shall tell him I am dead!

## THE DYING GIRL

Far away, he thinks me blooming
  Into beauty proud and dear,
While before my orbs are looming
  Visions of the shroud and bier.

Take these withered lilies to him—
  Whence this tremor, whence this gloom?
Show the buds, all drooping, show him—
  Let him strew them o'er my tomb.

Icy drops upon me gleaming —
  Slower, slower pants my breath;
Tell me, mother, am I dreaming—
  Tell me, am I tasting death?

I am going! I am going!
  Far from Harry—far from home,
Where eternal truth is glowing—
  Where the meteor angels roam.

The spoiler comes, on flashing pinions,
  Thirsting is his eager dart;
Now he beckons to his minions—
  Now his keen lance drinks my heart!

Farewell, father! farewell, mother!
  Catch my latest look and sigh;
Farewell, Harry—more than brother—
  God of life! I die—I die!

## JAMAIS

Early love is swift and golden,
  Fond and foolish, too, perchance,
But 'tis haloed by the olden,
  Golden moonlight of romance.
Once it's ripe aurelia bound me,
  Brimful with the birds of May;
By the ruins that surround me,
  It shall bind no more—Jamais!

Once I felt the blue above thee,
  Peri-peopled by thine art;
But 'twas death in life to love thee,
  Woman of the diamond heart!
Thou hast sown the sky with ashes,
  Made its constellations grey,
While the wind-gust knells and gnashes
  Dirge-like to the night—"Jamais!"

## JAMAIS

I was rich in pure affection,
  Passions chastened and alert —
But my rival had perfection
  In the opulence of—dirt.
He but wooed thee to deceive thee,
  Won thee, only to betray;
Shall that shadow ever leave thee?
  Never while I live—Jamais!

Time is just, and Fate's surrender
  Comes like chrism and myrrh to me.
He is quelled in coffined splendor,
  Hearsed in marble mimicry.
I—though Arctic years have chilled me,
  Thrust my stature in the day;
But the voice that erst has thrilled me,
  Thrills no more—Jamais! Jamais!

Though with purpose unbenighted,
  Though with intellect unshorn,
Still my spirit maimed and blighted,
  Bleeds beyond its battle morn.
Herbless deserts demon-haunted,
  Mark the fury of the fray,
But that spirit, still undaunted,
Bends to thee—Jamais! Jamais!

Woman! I shall cling beside thee
  As a marvel in thy way;
While I scorn, I shall deride thee
  With this requiem of "Jamais!"
Sleep—with adders on thy pillow—
  Wake—but spectral shapes of clay,
Flocking from the cloud and billow,
  Goad thee with—"Jamais!" "Jamais!"

---

## THE CAMEO BRACELET

Eva sits on the ottoman there,
  Sits by a Psyche carved in stone,
With just such a face and just such an air,
  As Esther upon her throne.

She's sifting lint for the brave who bled,
  And I watch her fingers float and flow
Over the linen, as thread by thread,
  It flakes to her lap like snow.

A bracelet clinks on her delicate wrist,
  Wrought, as Cellini's were at Rome,
Out of the tears of the amethyst
  And the wan Vesuvian foam.

And fall on the bauble-crest alway—
  A cameo image keen and fine—
Glares thy impetuous knife, Corday,
  And the Lara-locks are thine.

I thought of the wehr-wolves on our trail,
  Their gaunt fangs sluiced with gouts of blood;
'Til the Past, in a dead, mesmeric veil,
  Drooped with a wizard flood.

'Til the surly blaze, through the iron bars,
  Shot to the hearth, with a pang and cry—
And a lank howl plunged from the Champ de Mars
  To the Column of July.

'Til Corday sprang from the gem, I swear,
  And the dove-eyed damsel I knew had flown—
For Eva was not on the ottoman there,
  By Psyche carved in stone.

She grew like a Pythoness, flushed with fate,
  With the incantation in her gaze—
A lip of scorn, an arm of hate,
  And a dirge of the Marseillaise!

Eva, the vision was not wild,
  When wreaked on the tyrants of the land—
For you were transfigured to Nemesis, child,
  With the dagger in your hand!

## THE COBRA CAPELLO

"The cobra, though exceedingly venomous, has an aspect of gentleness and docility."—Encyclopedia.

Beautiful—yes! for her basilisk eyes
Gleam out when the features are luscious and mellow;
Beautiful—yes! but adown the disguise,
I detect just a tinge of the Cobra Capello.

And I think Mother Eve looked exactly like this
When she played such a prank on uxorious Adam;
I've a chronic dislike to a serpentine kiss,
And never eat apples in any style, Madam.

Beautiful—yes! as she paddles her fan
'Mid the bordered lagoons of her robe of white muslin;
And the tight little boot taps a quick rataplan,
In a way most piratical, not to say puzzling.

## THE COBRA CAPELLO

She prates of Tom Noddy, the handsome young goose
Of Don Trombonetti, divine on the flute;
And then, with a smile that's as arch as—the deuce,
Quotes pert panegyrics on somebody's foot!

She'll sing you a hymn or tell you a fib,
(Just one of those cynical, feathery trifles,)
And then, with a smirk that I think rather glib,
Sigh after some monster that left with the Rifles.

She vows I'm a miracle walking with men—
(Ugh! I swallow it all with a groan and a cough),
For I know that most women are comical, when
Their nightcaps are on and the visitors off!

Ay, rattle ahead and prattle away,
But, in sepulchred thought, I brood over another;
We parted, alas! about nine months today,
And we never must meet again—somehow or other.

They tell me, poor bird, it is painful to see
How you've changed, since we rode in the warm
summer weather;
And oh, if I felt you were pining for me,
I'd hew me a path that would bring us together.

In your solitude still, do you sing the old songs?
O, the "Long Weary Day!" shall it cease for us never?
But here, in the ruck of the sumptuous throngs,
Your name in my lone heart is sacred forever!

Ah me! I am chill, for 'tis fearful to sit
By the Cobra, when languished with tenderer matters—
Ha! I see that my secret is guessed—every bit—
For she's nibbling her lip, and the fan is in tatters.

Beautiful—yes! but I shall not succumb,
Though wifeless from Beersheba even to Dan;
Heigho! if my heart were but under her thumb,
She'd crumple it, too, like the innocent fan!

## WHY THE ROBIN'S BREAST IS RED

The Saviour, bowed beneath his cross,
  Clomb up the dreary hill,
While from the agonizing wreath
  Ran many a crimson rill.
The brawny Roman thrust him on
  With unrelenting hand—
Till, staggering slowly 'mid the crowd,
  He fell upon the sand.

A little bird that warbled near,
  That memorable day,
Flitted around and strove to wrench
  One single thorn away;
The cruel spike impaled his breast,
  And thus 'tis sweetly said,
The Robin wears his silver vest
  In panoplies of red.

Ah Jesu! Jesu! Son of Man!
  My dolour and my sighs
Reveal the lesson taught by this
  Winged Ishmael of the skies.
I, in the palace of delight,
  Or caverns of despair,
Have plucked no thorns from Thy dear brow,
  But planted thousands there!

## ADIEU

Adieu! adieu!
Bright eye of blue,
With ebbless oceans in thy hue;
Unloved, unblest,
I can not rest,
While thou art waving to the West.

His prayer surceased,
The Golden Priest
Hath chanted Masses in the East,
And soon will skim
The river's rim,
To sing his dying vesper hymn.

I think—I think
If I could sink
Beyond this juggling orbit's brink,
That I might drown
The Demon's frown,
Where suns and satellites go down.

## ADIEU

Farewell! farewell!
My bonnie belle,
I dungeon what I cannot quell;
Distraction's slave,
I weep and rave,
While prophets warn me from the grave.

A wretch abhorred,
I broke my sword
Upon the buckler of the Lord;
I feel the shock,
Upon my rock,
While the foul condors 'round me flock.

Good-bye! good-bye!
I can not die
Beneath thy sacramental eye;
When gulf and knoll
Atween us roll,
Wilt thou be patient then, my soul?

Adieu! adieu!
Sad eye of blue;
I've wrecked my life within thy hue.
I grieve, I grieve,
And yet I live
To know the future God may give.

I flee the plain,
Accurst by Cain,
To grasp my battle-ax again;
And in the sign
Of Bread and Wine
God the Consoler! I am Thine!

---

## SILVER SPRING

When the Lord of Light revealed
The flashing radiance of His shield,
Glorifying wave and field;
When he felt he must expire,
Then His orbs with blazing ire
Shot their dying shafts of fire;
When the palpitating breeze
Smote the gitterns of the trees,
Like the shout of distant seas;
When the jeweled birds that sing
Moved on rainbow-tinted wing,
I beheld thy face of splendor blushing with the wild
and tender,
Silver Spring!

## SILVER SPRING

Virgin! when the shadows roll
To the ice-embattled pole,
From thy sweet, pellucid soul—
Each angelic host on high
Sees in that cerulian eye
Blossom-beauties of the sky.
Blessed spirits! ye who dwell
Far beyond the ether swell,
How ye anthem, "It is well!"
On thy bosom let me seem
Kerneled in a Bagdad dream,
Rocked to slumber by a Seraph over thy celestial stream!

On a fairy, pensive pinion
Gloat I o'er thy deep dominion,
Shaming e'en the Augustinian;
Wonders rushing thicker—faster!
Here a porphyry pilaster,
Here a temple alabaster;
And the sunshine as it falls
Splinters on quintillion halls,
And a miracle of walls!
Now thy bannerets are beaming—
Now with mystic music gleaming
O'er a city—gem-girt city—in a gush of dervish dreaming!

Here, ah here, the Indian maiden,
When with love and languor laden,
Sought thee, as the cells of Adenn;
With a world of gentle guesses,
In thy flood her floating tresses
Poured their cascade of caresses!
Here her hero from the rattle
Of the crimson blows of battle,
Slept beneath her soothing prattle—
Slept—but, ere the sun's decline,
Like the lightning-riven pine,
And his heart's blood, Silver Billow, swept its throbbings into thine.

When the sad and solemn moon
Muses o'er the lone lagoon,
And laughs the melancholy loon,
When the crooning winter breeze,
Hapless from the Hebrides,
Chafes the dead cathedral trees;
'Mid the vultures muffled wails,
Stifled by the panther hails
Shuddering up palmetto trails;
When the globe is wrought in sleep,
When the gnomes their vigils keep
By the mountain and the deep—
I can fancy phantom things,
On their thunder-tarnished wings,
Soaring with a fallen grandeur over the enchanted springs!

## QUEEN OF THE WAX DOLLS

Dusky plume and siroc frown,
Lo the night comes trampling down
O'er thy palaces and town!
Lo! a legion like the stars,
Speeding from their crystal cars,
Leap beyond the sable bars;
How they glittered as they roll'd!
How thy streets are stormed with gold!
Undine! Undine! thou art princess of the parables
of old!

---

## TO THE QUEEN OF THE WAX DOLLS

'Twas in the old church yard I told you all,
Beneath the Norway pine;
There, by your mother's grave, I thought to call
That poor lost mother mine.

I saw you bend above an orphan child
To kiss its winsome face;
This woman, quoth I, is all undefiled,
A miracle of grace.

The world could never guess your riddle quite,
Nor shake your soft repose;
The same meek orbs that shone upon the night,
Were stars when morning rose.

Oh hypocrite! your cool, Antarctic sighs
Make memory an eclipse;
I feel the serpent from those poisoned eyes
Browsing upon my lips.

You *changed.* You stumbled from the better path;
You robed your vows on biers;
And now my lexicon of love and wrath
Is syllabled with tears.

You changed! Your eyes are purple-lidded beads,
Your hair a coil of flax,
And the cold splendor of your shape recedes
Into a mould of wax!

O, wormwood! that a thing of wax and wire
Could make me love it so;
I, with a Hecla-heart and nerve of fire,
Gasping amid that snow.

## QUEEN OF THE WAX DOLLS

And now, repenting, you would be my wife,
Would pawn your troth to *me*—
Poor Doll! beyond the icebergs of your life
There throbs no open sea!

I sought it once, and lo! my former self
Is shipwrecked in the quest.
See the impassioned Franklin, with his pelf,
Dead on your gelid breast.

You scream—'tis but a delicate doll's cry—
A trick, as all perceive it;
They say you're stuffed with sawdust—though a lie,
A skeptic might believe it!

---

## STONE APPLES

'Mid the shimmer of lamps and the redowa's dash,
Where the trumpet the thick-tongued song salutes--
'Mid the flutter of gauze and the diamond's flash,
'Mid the masquerade of flutes!

The boreal wind outside was keen,
  And the heavens had frosty eyes that night;
Within was the realm of a tropic queen,
  Auroral with delight.

Amiddle the foam of the frescoed ships
  On the pictured walls were the genii grim;
And the languid lotus, with chaliced lips,
  Was nectared to the brim.

Here bevies of blondes with hyacinth hair,
  Flirt their silver arms 'mid the fervid dance;
And the dusk-eyed brunette wreathes her snare
  Through the sensuous advance.

The vivid, voluptuous waltz is done,
  But the beaux are busy as they can be;
The buzzing butterflies round the sun
  Of a dazzling coterie.

But I, in the wavering whirl of mirth
  Cast gloom and glamour far and wide;
To me 'twas the emptiness of earth—
  The feast of the Barmecide.

## STONE APPLES

And there in a niche by the colonnade,
  Alone with the crisp and biting breeze,
I counted the curves by the river made,
  And the grenadier-like trees.

And I vow that the cold and dark to me
  Were better than melody, wit and wine,
For I saw, what never on earth should be,
  Under the chill moonshine.

I saw by the sinewy river side
  A willowy cottage, neat and white,
Where the bayou ripples prank and glide
  To the clover aleft and right.

And a damsel, shaming the damsels here,
  With nought of their satin and silk and pearls,
She—in a modest, maidenly sphere,
  They—like the Gwazee girls!

Oh, how I worshipped you then and there,
  The mother of God alone can tell—
With the bandeau dimming your starry hair,
  And your hand in mine, Estelle!

Lo! the boreal wind blew warm and soft,
  And the heavens had gentle eyes for all—
I looked, with a gallant smile, aloft,
  And my spirit had no gall.

My steps were turned to the ball again,
  With an arching front and a springy tread—
"Oh, *she* is an angel to this train;
  She is better than any," I said.

And better is she, sweet child, away
  In that willowy cottage, neat and white,
For she is the darlingest bird of day,
  But these are the birds of night.

The dear God nestles her eyes in sleep,
  And her visions are beautiful and serene;
The dawn has nothing for her to weep,
  With a flushed, disheveled mien.

And I swear, as I murmured things like these,
  And even the revelry seemed but good,
I saw, 'mid its giddiest ecstacies,
  My Violet of the Wood.

## STONE APPLES

Not in the garb of the olden days,
  But tricked with a tinselry of toys—
And she frowned as she met my eager gaze,
  And she smiled o'er the foppish joys.

And she, high and haughtily, brushed me by,
  To harvest the spoils of her fevered bliss—
To drink in the honeyed laugh and lie,
  The honeyed serpent's hiss.

Yes! the boreal wind cut keen and bleak,
  And the heavens had frosty eyes once more,
For the apples I plucked from the Venus-cheek
  Were petrified to the core!

And I sighed to my heart: "My love is rash,
  Since these are the false and blasting fruits;
I thrust it back 'mid the diamond's flash,
  'Mid the masquerade of flutes"!

## ALTHEE

Could tongue define
In warbling line
The music of this heart of mine,
'Twould sing, today,
A roundelay,
For thee, ma belle Creole Althee!

But words are weak,
When words would speak,
The ripeness of thy satin cheek,
Or pearl that tips
With dewy sips
The arches of those blushing lips.

The floods of lace
That flirt and race
In eddying ripples 'round thy face,
Have framed, I ween,
In magic mien,
The daintiest image ever seen.

## ALTHEE

Ah, sweet Althee!
Around thee play
The plumed, and crystal tribes of May;
And in those eyes
Float, flash, and rise
Gay atmosphere of orient guise.

The eyes—the eyes!
The planet eyes
Fresh from their dreams of Paradise!
My spirit sees,
But never flees
Their sorcery of sorceries.

Truth, Grace, and Love
From worlds above—
Hints of the Pure and Holy Dove—
Divinely bright,
These gems of sight
Are throned upon their globes of light.

Thus heaven-beguiled,
Beloved child,
Have all the cherubs on thee smiled;
Let joys depart
Still, sweet, thou art
Voiced in the virgin's sacred heart.

Madonna! fold
Her heart of gold
In thy dear arms, when it is cold;
Madonna! sing
This bird of Spring
To sleep beneath thy velvet wing!

Athwart my brain
A shadowy rain
Sobs forth this desolate refrain:
*Thy star is sped,*
*Thy sunshine fled,*
*Thy dream is bosomed with the dead!*

Ay! dim—dim—dim—
My senses swim
Down by the lordly river's brim;
All pagan-eyed,
I thrust my pride
Out on the mad and stalwart tide.

And will it roll
To some fair goal,
Quaffing elixirs of the soul—
Or witheringly
Grope out to sea
And drift—but will it drift to thee?

# ISIS

## ISIS

My friend, the young artist, is clever and kind,
With a broad Roman forehead and deep German heart;
And though but a tyro, I cannot be blind
To his whimsical skill and his exquisite art.

I laugh at his quips, as I lounge in his room,
Where we gin the grum world with its duns and its debts,
Till spun by philosophy out of the gloom,
And Calle Obispo's divine cigarettes.

Anon we play chess, with the odds of a pawn,
On an arabesque baize full of goblins and Circes;
You should see how he strangles a masculine yawn
As I gasp out my last little spasm of verses.

'Tis the game of my life, this game of the squares,
For my Queen of White Chessmen is coy as the stars;
When a bishop, like Dunstan, snakes up unawares
And soon there is nothing but death—or cigars!

Cotillions of smoke swirl the curtains and walls
  By a swart old Tertullian, all gnarled and knotty;
And then in quadrilles, as it stifles and crawls
  On a muscular torso by Buonarotti.

Here Leviathan gores through a shock of harpoons—
  There, Lazarus mumbles his crust on the sod—
Afar, in this carnival dance of cartoons,
  Hypatia glares on the crucified God!

Here, Scanderberg gashes the Ottomite van—
  There, the dulcimer damsel of Kubla is heard—
Hard by, a neat sketch of the crafty old man
  We have sent to inveigle Napoleon the Third.

There are foils on the arras and shields on the stair,
  While an arquebuse bosses the lank balustrade;
And trailing just over that worm-eaten chair
  Is a woman's white dress with its bodice and braid.

The visions of youth are the wizards of thought,
  No matter how gusty, no matter how good;
How many have married the woman they sought—
  How seldom we marry the woman we should!

## ISIS

I sprang from the couch, till I stood by the side
  Of my friend, as he gazed at the bodice and dress;
"This way," whispered he, "and I'll show you a bride
  Not to wed but to worship—to sing not to bless."

Dear God! as the picture the painter unsealed,
  The curtain was shrivelled away to a scroll—
I felt that an Isis of Eld was revealed,
  That Isis I veiled in the crypt of my soul!

Those pure melting eyes float that mystical gauze,
  Which prophecy weaves on the sight and the hair
Of those that peer down the death-vistas and pause
  O'er the slab and the violets waiting them there.

There's a fountain of tears by the fountain of mirth,
  As twilights are thin 'twixt an old and new leaven;
And if not a paladin hero of earth
  She could make me a passionate pilgrim of heaven.

Ah, the glove's on the mantel, the rose in the glass,
  The name in the Bible upon the blank page,
And the very same rosary fingered at mass
  Coiled by the canary bird—dead in its cage.

O beautiful child of a beautiful morn!
There's a beautiful bodice begemming thy breast,
But it speaks of the cerement, that Seraphs have worn,
And it tells of a nightingale slain in its nest.

And I gaze, and I gaze, and I gaze, 'till the moon,
With its irised aureola, sleeps on her brow—
My Isis! thy image departed too soon,
For I gaze and I gaze on thy vacancy now.

O beautiful child of a beautiful day!
There's a beautiful song on thy Sibylline lip;
But it sings of the breaker that boils in the bay,
And it dirges the doom of a desolate ship.

Lost—lost, long ago! and she dreams o'er the sea,
Where the rude Saxon daisies above her have blown;
I know that the angels are angry with me,
For the woman is dead that my spirit hath known!

*New Orleans*, 1861.

COLONEL JAMES RYDER RANDALL
(In 1882)

## FAR OUT AT SEA

## FAR OUT AT SEA

Far out at sea! far out at sea!
  The winged wind warbles melody;
The billows fringe their curls of foam,
  And tremble back with thoughts of home;
I stream my soul on every crest
  That gambles onward to the west—
'Tis freighted, love, with hope and thee.

Far out at sea! far out at sea!
  The petrels soar the surge with glee;
The livelong day they skim the air,
  The livelong night they slumber there—
Wild, wand'ring souls of those who sleep
  Beneath the coral-citied deep,
And from the shades heart-break to be
  Far out at sea! far out at sea!

Far out at sea! far out at sea!
  The bird-like bark flew merrily!
The day-god slept—his bride on high
  Wove isles of light o'er wave and sky;
On, on we flew, and from the wake
  What moon-enameled beauties break!
A vapory veil of silver bars
  Entangled in a sky of stars—
Supernal visions came to me
  Far out at sea! far out at sea!

Far out at sea! far out at sea!
  The raven screams upon the lee;
The storm-king rides the lightning now,
  And wreck and ruin bare his brow—
A gallant ship, descending fast,
  Is whirled beneath the waters vast,
And with her in the whelming tide,
  The loveliest child that ever died
In faith, in purity and pride!
One fair white arm upon her breast,
  One sunny curl lost from the rest,
And there she lies—sweet Melanie!
  Far out at sea! far out at sea!

## FLOURINE

Far out at sea! far out at sea!
  And art thou happy, Melanie?
Oh! in thy grand and mystic grave
  Beneath the blue, blue tropic wave,
Dost see, sweet child, the diamond blaze
  Upon the Nereid of old days—
Dost hear the choral song of shells,
  More musical than golden bells—
  And in thy ocean jubilee
Dost think of him who loveth thee?
  Far out at sea! far out at sea!

---

## FLOURINE

Little Flourine, with golden hair,
And rose-red cheeks and features fair,
You shall be the New Year's Queen,
                Little Flourine!

Pretty Flourine, with the bright-blue eyes,
Whose tints are caught from the azure skies;
Airy, fairy, with heavenly mien,
                Pretty Flourine!

Dainty Flourine, with your dazzling grace,
And the beautiful wonders of your face;
May you have nothing but roses to glean,
Dainty Flourine!

Darling Flourine, may Time bring to you
Days full of music and skies full of blue—
Bliss that the saints and the angels have seen,
Darling Flourine!

---

## ALEXANDRINE

'Twas the morning of Palm Sunday, in Village Adair,
And the shy little chapel seemed jubilant there;
'Twas the morn of Palm Sunday, sad Sunday, I ween
That I met thee and loved thee, Alexandrine, Alexandrine!

I stood by the pew that was nearest to thine,
While gentle St. Agnes, just over the shrine,
Yearned tenderly to thee, as if she had seen,
Thy face up in Heaven, Alexandrine, Alexandrine!

## ALEXANDRINE

I remember thy bodice, so snowy and blest,
With a violet guarding its virginal nest;
Thy sensitive forehead, thy contour serene,
And a ripple of ringlets, Alexandrine, Alexandrine!

We met in the aisle—how I think of it now!
And meekly I tendered my sanctified bough.
'Twas fondled, thy darling, deft fingers between—
*Ah! the poor bough is withered,* Alexandrine,
Alexandrine!

And withered am I by a pitiless doom,
Like a blast from the lungs of the Demon Simoon;
In the magical spell of a haunted ravine,
Dost thou hear when I call thee, Alexandrine?
Alexandrine!

On my cheek there is health, all my mind is aglow,
But my soul is the saddest Sahara, I know;
For thought hath not compassed, and eye hath not
seen
The kingdom I'm banished from, Alexandrine,
Alexandrine!

By the way of the cross gleams thy radiant crown;
By the way of the world all my dreams have gone
down:
For thee peace and mercy; for me daggers keen,
And war with the wehr-wolf, Alexandrine,
Alexandrine!

In thy saintliest prayer I would ask to remain,
Though for me there be no resurrection again.
The stars in their courses have mocked me, my
queen,
But I bless thee forever, Alexandrine, Alexandrine!

Thy sorrows were many, thy happy days few;
Thy tears bowed thee down like a rose crushed
with dew;
But those tears were too precious for mortal to
glean,
And a bride of the sky art thou, Alexandrine,
Alexandrine!

SPEAKING EYES

## SPEAKING EYES

There are some faces, rarely met,
  That weave a weird and winsome spell,
Just as the songs we ne'er forget
  Of Kubla Khan and Christabel;
And these—so strange and fine—eclipse
  The silken swarm of rosebud dyes—
Though silence loiters on the lips,
  Sad poems warble with the eyes.

And such a face, sweet child, is thine,
  Thine in the blossom of thy days—
Ah! woe is me! that love of mine
  Should nestle in that magic gaze!
We met but once, and 'mid my brain
  The flames of sorcery arise—
Oh! should we ever meet again,
  Speak to me, darling, with thine eyes!

Through many lands I sought to find
  Some idol nobler than the Past;
No more a pilgrim pale and blind,
  I've found thee, loveliest, at last!
At last, I scan thy warm, white brow,
  At last, the Mecca planets rise—
The wizard charm is on me now—
  Speak to me, darling, with thine eyes!

And with thine eyes, beloved, speak
  The subtle thought that keeps me strong,
The sacred hope that fires my cheek
  In combat with the base and wrong.
Better the everlasting night
  Than glittering with the world's disguise,
But while the Heaven is in their light,
  Speak to me, darling, with thine eyes!

My days are dark, and still I think
  To claim thee in this globe of ours—
Brimming the swart Vesuvian brink
  Volcanic brows are fringed with flowers;
Together, by eternal meads
  That broaden up to healthier skies,
My heart shall answer with its deeds
  What thou art speaking with thine eyes!

*Written in* 1863.

## THE GRAND DUKE

You gave me flowers in the crimson eves,
  Down by the garden gate,
Where, on his throne of glad geranium leaves,
  The Grand Duke sat in state.

You pitied him—the Grand Duke—and you sent
  A rare and budding bride,
A lithe and fragrant Duchess, dew-be-sprent,
  Snow-bosomed and blue-eyed.

Anon, the Grand Duke frowned and stood apart—
  The cold and bashful churl!
Until you bound them, darling, heart to heart,
  With one enamored curl.

Ah me! I have the plaintive bouquet here,
  With all its lustre fled;
The lissome bride on her geranium bier,
  And the dear Grand Duke—dead.

And many sad and sombre thoughts arise
  Within me and without;
Spectres of flowerets pictured on mine eyes,
  Robed in a shroud of doubt.

Here, in the hot June midnight, grave and lone,
  By the dull candle's flare,
I weave unutterable words, and moan
  Over a woman's hair.

"Only a woman's hair!" and still I sob
  O'er memory with her pearls,
Crushing my brows with anguish till they throb—
  Writhing my soul with curls.

No—no! I must not ponder things like these;
  Be mine a breast of mail—
Though but a Nautilus of frenzied seas,
  Swift—solitary—frail.

The world will know you not, my song, for you
  Speak but to one, and say
Something I dare not, to an eve of blue
  When I am far away.

I dare not—for I flit the waif of chance,
  A riddle few have read,
Like the Grand Duke, I've had my day's romance,
  Like the Grand Duke, am dead.

MY BONNY KATE

## MY BONNY KATE!

The sultry sun with angry eye,
  Gleams from the lurid summer sky,
Through all the veins of red July,
          My bonny Kate!
So, very sad and very lone,
  I sit beside the window stone
Musing on months forever flown,
          My bonny Kate!

This very day, one year ago,
  I roamed where Charleston fronts the foe,
And loved, but did not tell you so,
          It was my fate.
But soon I sought your eager eyes
And answered all their glad surprise
With love that falters not nor dies,
          My bonny Kate!

You must remember times so bright
When every pulse thrilled through with light,
Watching the sweet morn's silver flight,
My bonny Kate!
That evening in the country town,
The morning ride, up hill and down,
The spring, where Eros won his crown,
My bonny Kate!

We parted, 'twas the first sharp pain,
We met and parted once again—
It seemed as though our love were vain,
So long to wait!
I strove to bring the world to bay,
From early dawn to twilight grey.
The promised land loomed far away,
My bonny Kate!

Thus garnered, in that sacred past,
My love has grown superb and vast,
Each day sublimer than the last,
My bonny Kate!
My heart is full and yet I know,
To-morrow it will overflow,
Forever yours, for weal or woe,
My bonny Kate!

Then, darling, think what pangs assail
Your lover's triple vest of mail,
Dreaming that even you might fail,
    Your last year's mate.
Another sits where you have been,
With you another walks the green
And tender words have passed between,
    My bonny Kate!

A few short weeks, and I may be
Dashing along the hostile sea,
Winning the gold that ransoms thee,
    My bonny Kate!
To God I yield the doubt—to you
I give my solemn troth anew,
My love, my faithful and my true—
    My bonny Kate!

## ELSIE GAY

You gave me a geranium leaf—
  A little thing but full of meaning;
When inclinations half belief,
  The token made it worth the gleaning.
Last night your hand was clasped in mine,
  'Twas but the pressure of a minute,
And yet, by some mysterious sign,
  A red rose blushed to birth within it!

Oh! rather pluck for me, fair child
  A branch of cypress or of willow;
My days are bleak, my thoughts are wild,
  I am but sea-weed on the billow.
For me nor love, nor home, nor wife
  Can ever be a curse or blessing—
The envious riddle of my life
  Would puzzle half your days in guessing.

A week—a month—perchance a year,
  You might remember how you met me,
And then, with neither smile nor tear,
  'Twill be so easy to forget me.
With you the world is frolic May,
  With me, 'tis many a month of weeping—
And you'll be dancing, Elsie Gay
  When I am in the valley sleeping.

## THE WILLOW

"Et moi, j'ai aussi été en Arcadie"

My parent stem was nurtured in the soil
  Of St. Helena, near the grave of him
Who shook the world in many a battle-broil,
  And died a captive where dark waters swim,
In that lone isle of Afric's subtle coil—
  A memory no time or age may dim.

Torn from that ever memorable tree,
  I was borne long and weary miles away,
Across a mighty waste of restless sea,
  To be enrooted in the honored clay
That guards the noblest son of Liberty
  Asleep, awaiting the eternal day.

So, after mingling with heroic dust—
  Napoleon, Washington—I came at last
To find a final resting place, I trust;
  Where the Savannah's tawny tide glides past
A city venerable and august—
  In a glad garden I was fondly cast.

I bravely grew, wooed by a Southern sun,
  A graceful tree, with opulence of tress.
The vital sap through all my fibers spun,
  And dainty damsels gave me their caress.
A lovely matron all my senses won,
  And so I longed her happy home to bless.

Anon, the winter stripped me of my leaves,
  Until I stood disheveled and forlorn;
But still my tropic heart clung to the eaves
  Of that dear household, in the night and morn.
Soon the lord Spring, who blesses and reprieves,
  Poured emerald largess o'er my features shorn.

How have I thrilled when they I loved were gay,
  In the warm sunshine and the alert breeze!
When round the festal board wit ruled the day
  And wisdom was espoused to pleasantries.
How have I wished such happiness could stay,
  Unsmitten always with sad memories!

Alas! there came a dread, dissolving scene
  To snap the jocund circle of my friends!
So, one by one, they fled all things terrene,
  To seek the mystic shore that never ends—
Where Mortal must on th' Immortal lean,
  Where the true Ideal with the Real blends.

## THE WILLOW

The reverend grandsire left my grateful shade
  And baby eyes beheld my form no more;
The dazzling lawyer in the sod was laid;
  The keen preceptor fell, with all his lore;
The brilliant master slumbers in the glade—
  Not lost, but in due meekness gone before.

Still lingers my sweet matron, gravely bright,
  With stalwart sons and daughters tall and grand.
They stand between her and the ghosts who might
  Become a mournful, melancholy band.
I watch her, when the hours are aflight,
  Her gaze uplifted to the shining strand!

  Perchance, you think a willow has no tongue,
  No sentient touch, no article of speech,
No power to soothe the heart, in anguish wrung,
  No message to impart or moral teach.
But lo! a poet all my dreams has sung,
  And who that sorcery will dare impeach?

## ARCHITECTURE

Gone—gone the spires, and pinnacles, and fanes,
  I built upon the mist-isles of the past,
Nought but a hollow Babylon remains
  Of all the bright, adorable, and vast;
Still I make miraculous amends
By hewing Meccas from your hearts, my friends!

Welcome! ye passionate rills that cleave my brain,
  Blest with ebullient melodies of morn—
While 'mid the plumed battalia of the cane
  Throb the red sun-flags by encrimsoned corn!
Here, where the forest with the field contends,
I'll sculpture immortalities, my friends!

Imperial Heart! that blossomed into mine
  Hot with eleusia of electric youth—
Friend of my boyhood! a majestic shrine
  I chisel from that burning heart of truth.
Where the parched gulls to velvet waves descend,
Be thou, my Monolith of Faith, my friend!

## ARCHITECTURE

Devoted Heart! that bore mine, like an ark,
  Through the blind deluge of disease and care,
Giving it shelter in the light when dark
  And hideous fortunes throttled with despair—
While the glad planets o'er the globe impend,
Be thou my battlement of Pride, my friend!

Undaunted Heart! that into mine hath poured
  The subtle wine-blood of its lusty praise—
A living bulwark, with its shield and sword,
  When I had fallen upon coward days;
O, could I to ethereal worlds ascend,
Thy Heart should be my Pantheon, my friend!

Maternal Heart! that charmed mine in the path
  That glideth to the splendor of the Throne,
And soothed it, blistered in the climes of wrath,
  And kissed it, shud'ring from the abyss of moan,
The sweet, sweet skies, like incense, interblend
About the Altar of thy Heart, my friend!

And *thou*—who comest like a meteor-beam
  To quell me in the zenith of my pride—
Thou—thou who mocketh me with that fatal gleam
  Which gave me but the ghost-world for a bride—
Woe! woe! the palaces I wrought depart,
And all my necromancy is a tomb—my Heart.

## MARATHON

Written at the Age of Eighteen

Stern Marathon! the mountains view thee yet;
Thy monarch plain with dew eternal's wet!
Each blade of grass that feathers from thy green
Bears the bright impress of a hallowed mien.
Shoot to the sky their cloud-defiant crest
The bristling rocks, with climbing vines caressed;
Cradle the King-bird in his eyrie home,
When down he darts from heaven's starry dome;
Stand the bold sentries of the holy vast;
Hurl from their thrones the thunder-throated blast;
Sigh o'er the graves of valorous renown;
Then lordly smile whilst gazing grandly down—
Tomb of the Brave! thy echo sways the breeze,
Before thy name all mimic grandeur flees,
Before thy fame the world is thrilled with awe,
Time has no tooth—Oblivion rends its maw!
Those martyr forms whom ages cannot quell
Haunt the grey sod whereon they grap'ling fell—
Call from the dust the Persian's fiery host,
And lo! what tumult stirs each gibbering ghost!
Thus when the lurid bolt is whirled along,
These grim old foes are mingled once again:

## MARATHON

When the hoarse thunder bellows from the sky,
And dusky pinions storm the cliffs on high;
When the big rain comes rattling from the clouds
Starting the dead in myriads from their shrouds—
Amid the clangor of their dread refrain
These grim old foes are mingled once again:
The dark Platean in the tide of war,
The comely Median in his battered car,
The bright Athenian dealing death and fear,
The Persian tottering on his shivered spear—
The cloven helmet and the ghastly blow,
The crimson scimetar, the stringless bow—
They smite their shields, they form, prepare, advance:
Sword splinters sword, lance crashes against lance—
Away! the golden lamp swings forth once more
And all is mute upon that dreamy shore!

The living hills are marble for the dead,
Their burial ground is where they fought and bled,
Their epitaph is centred in a breath—
"The dying freeman yields not quite to death!"
Their deeds are chanted by the choral surge,
That holiest Harper of undying dirge!
Each frolic wave that pillows on the plain
Murmurs a praise surpassing mortal strain,
For those who perished there—but not in vain!

## ODE TO PROFESSOR DIMITRY

Suggested by his admirable lecture on the "Temples and Monuments of Greece"

Written at Georgetown University at the Age of Eighteen

Behold the man! What matchless lines of grace
Are blazoned round his great, expressive face!
The voice so full, so tremulously grand
Speaks from his heart the woes of that far land,
Which fallen now, once reigned the titled Queen
Of Mind, of Soul—all-seeing and all-seen—
Nurse of the Gods! bright Liberty's abode!
The Poet's pride! whence Homer's song has flowed,
Rolling with ocean-flow from age to age—
The first—the last—the best on History's page!
Foremost in Art, in Science, and in Strife,
In columned grandeur and in marble life—
Bend, bend before Hellenic tow'ring might
Ye gifted children of the Pure and Bright!
All this and more thrills forth—how silent all!
The burning echo riots round the hall,

## ODE TO PROFESSOR DIMITRY

In every breast responsive echoes breathe,
The ravished senses twine a deathless wreath
For those who fought for Freedom, scorning shame,
Then bartered life for an eternal fame!
Thus, not in vain, he courts the willing ear—
Calls on the dead, and living forms appear;
Both gods and men in awful grandeur move—
The "Blind old Bard"—the "Cloud-compelling Jove!"
He bids them tell of days when Greece was free,
When Athens rode triumphant o'er the sea,
Athens the peerless—prescient—the blind—
Athens the mutable—the undefined!
The fount of Eloquence! whose spring inspired
Her godlike son, and with his breath expired;
Which in one warning yet majestic cry
Made Philip quail and cowards gladly die!
When Sparta stalked the Lioness of the shore
With iron nerves—brute heart—what, nothing more?
Ay! ay! a single boon kind Nature gave,
Alone to drag her from Oblivion's grave;
One hoary rock, the Keystone of the plain—
A shivered altar but a hallowed fane,
For patriot's blood has trickled round the stone—
Dread august sacrifice! this—this alone

Redeems the land with a renewing birth,
Its faults forgotten in thy faultless worth!
Manes of the brave! your gore's not vainly shed—
O stern baptism on a nation's head!
Yet did that blood quench Persia's fiery pride
And seal the spot where heroes fell—not died,
Leaving thy name a watchword to the free—
Unmouldering Record! lone Thermopylae!
Turn from this scene. Exulting to the skies
A temple flits before the captive eyes,
Unrivalled, chaste e'en as the new-born day,
In perfect form it looms along the way—
Unrivalled whole—unrivalled in decay!
Behold the Parthenon—the miracle—the fair!
Look once again. What ruin breedeth there!
A pilfered wreck, a desecrated shrine,
Sport of the blast, polluted yet divine—
The mind untouched from a dismembered whole—
How glorious yet, thou Mecca of the Soul!

# HA! HA!

## HA! HA!

When summer suns are glancing on the merry damsels dancing
'Neath the pendulous aroma of the beauty-blushing vine;
When summer birds are cooing, in a pantomimic wooing
'Mid the azure-dimpled ether, which the poet calls divine:
I win a frolic girl,
From the rustle and the whirl,
And I say she is a seraph and I swear she is a pearl—
Ha! Ha!
Ha! Ha!
Who is gentler, who is fairer, ha! ha! who is sweeter,
Who is brighter, ha! ha! who is wittier and neater,
Than the queen of my spirit—its glorified defeater—
Ha! Ha! Ha! Malgherita! Malgherita!

Ha! gaily we are flying, with laughter, love and sighing,
O'er the valley of Berilla, in its livery of green!
Ha! madly we are dashing by the torrent thunder-flashing,

And beyond the echo-flutter of the flute and violin.
Little fairy, little fay,
From the torrent keep away,
Or thy roses and thy ribbons will be waltzing in the spray,
Ha! Ha!
Ha! Ha!
Who is gentler, who is fairer—ha! ha! who is sweeter;
Who is brighter, ha! ha! who is wittier and neater,
Than the queen of my spirit—its glorified defeater—
Ha! Ha! Ha! Malgherita! Malgherita!

In the twinkle of a minute, she wildly pours within it
The glory of her tresses like a vivid golden veil;
In a second of derision, she forgetteth her precision,
And is captured by the current as it dashes to the vale.
I shoot beneath the flood
All the lightning of my blood—
I reach her and I save her and I bear her to the wood.
Ha! Ha!
Ha! Ha!
Who is gentler, who is fairer—ha! ha! who is sweeter;

## HA! HA!

Who is brighter, ha! ha! who is wittier and neater,
Than the queen of my spirit—its glorified defeater—
Ha! Ha! Ha! Malgherita! Malgherita!

You may fancy that the fountain, baffled billow of the mountain,
Is singing you this secret as it crashes grandly down;
"What beatitude completer, he is wed to Malgherita,
And they emulate the angels 'neath the summer's burning crown!"
We are wed! we are wed!
As Khuleborn hath said,
And we envy not the annals of the living or the dead.
Ha! Ha!
Ha! Ha!
Who is gentler, who is fairer—ha! ha! who is sweeter;
Who is brighter, ha! ha! who is wittier and neater,
Than the queen of my spirit—its glorified defeater—
Ha! Ha! Ha! Malgherita! Malgherita!

## SARCASTIC

Loud sir, I am
—Myself o'er thrown
By your tremendous racket;
But let us see
In what degree
That you and I most lack it.

A wise old saw
Hath made it law—
(Now all your ears displaying)
That lions quell
Their roar a spell,
When jackasses are a-braying.

# MADAME LA GRIPPE

MADAME LA GRIPPE

Where the seas meet the land, and the land quits the
seas,
The universe shakes with a terrible sneeze,
The Czar in his palace, the serf in his hut,
Explode all alike when the nostril is shut,
The saint's holy person is no more exempt
Than the sinner whom Satan refuses to tempt.
The pest of the air takes a world-waking trip,
And its banners are blazoned: *"Beware of La
Grippe."*

We heard of it first where Peter the Great
Made the marsh of the Neva the heart of his State.
It crumpled the Cossack, and then, in the morn,
Crossed the Balkan and captured the fair Golden
Horn.
The Sultan dropped down with a bigness of head
That made his whole harem afraid of the dead,
For a microbic Skobeleff rushed with a skip
And held old Byzantium fast in his grip.

From the dome of Sophia to Stephen's tall spire
It swept in its fury and coughed in its ire.
The Kaiser succumbed before set of sun
And cried: "Better far Kossuth or the Hun!"
But the Hun was himself loaded up with quinine,
While Bismarck felt humbled at Canossa's shrine,
For the head of the haughty takes a cyclonic dip
When it feels the congestion of *Madame La Grippe!*

The Berlin professors went down in despair
And their scholars tore Greek, by the roots, from
their hair,
The Titans who humbled the nations are weak,
While their battle-cry sinks to a sad nasal squeak.
The Emperor William grows weary of beer,
And wiltedly "ambles away on his ear."
The White Lady scare and the pale Phantom Ship
Are nothing in horror like *Madame La Grippe!*

It tweaked the Republic of France by the nose,
And a new reign of terror insistently rose.
The dust of Napoleon quivered perhaps
With the cruel, catarrhal, convulsive collapse.
The Socialist demon declined to conspire,
For his backbone was seared by St. Anthony's fire.
The sirens who smile to beguile on the road
Felt their jewels a curse, like the head of a toad,

MADAME LA GRIPPE

And the doctor alone, who is sure of his tip,
Stood firm in the presence of *Madame La Grippe!*

Zigzagging along the Baltic's bleak strand,
It crossed the grim channel to sturdy England.
The eloquent Gladstone lost power of speech
And Salisbury took to his bed with a screech.
The Queen drank hot toddy of fine Irish make,
And dreamed that Parnell was attending her wake
With a dark, scowling visage and sinister lip,
Disguised in the raiment of *Madame La Grippe!*

Astride of the cable, by British emprise,
It shot to the land of the free and the wise.
The Bostonese stomach disdained pork and beans,
And lived on a diet of antipyrines.
New York heard the figure of Liberty whoop
Like a child in the robust embrace of the croup.
Mr. Chauncey Depew wrote funeral verse
While the Negro Problem passed by in a hearse.
The scissors were dropped from Coupon's keen clip
As Wall Street went mad in the waltz of *La Grippe!*

On the wings of a blizzard, it flew to the West,
With a wild and a woolly rheumatic behest.
Chicago surrendered at once the World's Fair
And took a first prize in the Prince of the Air.

Mr. Ingall's trumpet made all Kansas wheeze
As Washington answered his cynical sneeze.
The big bulk of Barnes was a rampart of might,
But it sunk at the shock of this malefic sprite.
East and West, West and East, with a roar and a rip,
Crashed the thunderous footfall of *Madame La Grippe!*

You may hear that this imp is a myth at the South,
But this is a pleasant romance of the mouth.
By the river St. John, at a place they call Jax,
This writer first felt the prelude of attacks.
Very mild was the touch, but as he fared forth,
A little more near to the stars of the North,
It kicked and it cuffed and it swirled him about
Until he resembled a famous dish-clout.
And now, as he takes his medicinal nip,
He bows out, most humbly, this *Madame La Grippe!*

The moral, perchance, is not proper to hide,
It levels at once our poor human pride.
We are all in the clutch of invisible foes,
And the elements fill us with blessings and woes.
We have brotherhood bonds to pay at our ease,
In all the vast circle of health and disease.
We are saved by the self-same Omnipotent Power,
While none is too poor to escape from its dower;
And little it matters, whatever may slip,
So God's buckler shield us from Satanic grip!

## SILHOUETTE

Ladies and gallants, well a day!
If ride ye must, and will not stay,
Ah, do not ride in midmost May!

Lassie! be sure to take your brother;
Laddie! go not without grandmother;
Lassie and laddie, take no other!

For I have been the dupe of blisses—
My malison on blonden Misses,
With cherry months lip-full with kisses;

And jaunty hats with ribboned bows,
And beaded basques and—heaven knows
What gilded pitfalls full of woes!

Dear little bread and butter chit,
You jilted me I must admit—
And split my heart—the deuce a bit!

I swore the jewel of Glamschid
Than you less excellency hid;
You thought so too—you know you did.

And yet you made a famous fool
Of one a lastrum since from school;
I'm on the penitential stool.

With groan and grimace acrimonious,
I vote all flirting most erroneous,
And bivouac with Saint Antonius,

Old Nick shall thump me black and blue,
And with his horned head punch me through,
Ere I succumb to jays like you.

I'll make the calaboose my bunk,
I'll delve in some monastic trunk;
'Twere highly proper to get drunk!

I'll sing *Am Rhein* in the Casino—
Become obstreperous with Blineau;
In divers ways I'll breeze my spleen, oh!

Lycanthropy to me is placid;
I'll out-strut e'en Haroun Alraschid—
Read Werter, too, for prussic acid.

## SILHOUETTE

I'll button-hole old Villabobia,
Prating of bonnets and Zenobia—
Bombastes B and hydrophobia.

Of Fremont—Brutus (Junius Lucius)—
Seward—Scæzola (baptized Mutius)—
Of Mother Goose and Kean Confucius.

All womankind shall learn to rue it;
I'll drench my locks with mutton suet,
And guard the corners—young men do it!

Upon reflection, I will *not*
Become an interesting sot,
And sprout a nasal apricot!

Philosophy shall be obeyed;
I'll puff my meerschaum in the shade,
And live to see you *an old maid!*

A starch old maid with snuff and chat,
With crippled curls and—think of that—
A fusty parrot and—a cat!

Alack! and what shall I be then?
Perchance a Bedouin with men—
Perchance a starved wolf in my den.

No—no! I can not hate you yet,
While many a treasured amulet
Of lang syne dares me to forgot!

I have your tiny gloves hard by;
You gave them to me with a sigh—
They're torn and faded—so am I.

I banquet on them with my looks,
I haunt the meadow—tangled brooks,
And sift dried jasmins from my books.

And brooding o'er them wrath is felled;
I only see the hands they held,
Becking me ever back to Eld!

Yes—yes! I *do* forgive the Past;
And though your stars be overcast,
I'll deem you loveliest to the last.

But I shall ride no more away,
In kingly cavalier array,
In midmost love—in midmost May!

## MAGDALEN

The Hebrew girl, with flaming brow,
  The banner-blush of shame,
Sinks at the sinless Saviour's knees
  And dares to breathe His name.
From the full fountain of her eyes
  The lava-globes are roll'd—
They wash his feet; she spurns them off
  With her ringlet-scarf of gold.

The Meek One feels the eloquence
  Of agonizing prayer,
The burning tears, the suppliant face,
  The penitential hair;
And when, to crown her brimming woe,
  The ointment box is riven—
"Rise, daughter, rise! Much hast thou loved,
  Be all thy sins forgiven!"

Dear God! The prayers of good and pure,
  The canticles of light,
Enrobe Thy throne with gorgeous skies,
  As incense in Thy sight;
May the shivered vase of Magdalen
  Soothe many an outcast's smart,
Teaching what fragrant pleas may spring
  From out a *broken heart!*

## KEATS

"Here lies one whose name was writ on water"

Beyond the wall that belts the town,
Where grand Saint Peter's titan crown
Looks apostolically down;

With shrunken form and shrouded lid,
The Song Bird—not the Song—is hid
Near Caius Cestius' pyramid.

There purer from his Roman pyre,
The star-eyed Skylark of the Choir,*
Slumbers, a radiant Child of Fire!

Twin bards—twin death! no slander parts,
With livid tongue and venomed darts,
The Soul of Souls and "Heart of Hearts."

The coheirs of Porphyrogene,
Their dreams are royal and serene
Beneath the Night's sweet sybil queen.

*Shelley.

## KEATS

Methinks, their sad song sadly calls
From every breeze that swells and falls
Along the Coliseum's halls.

And that sad song shall murmur there,
Upon the pulses of the air,
With incense-wings of warbled prayer.

And it shall sigh and fondly flit
When dome and tomb are bright moonlit,
O'er him whose name was water-writ.

'Twas writ on water, but the wave
That surges from a hallowed grave
Is not old Ocean's liquid slave.

'Tis the tumultuous Sea of Song—
The Scroll of the Anointed Throng
To whom eternities belong!

Thy name, dear Keats, had water-birth,
And now, in its majestic worth,
It heaves its billows over earth!

## PALINODIA

Though it leave me ashes, I will thrust
  This Etna from my breast,
My times have been tumultuous, they shall know
    The ecstacy of rest.

They marred the work of heaven when they scoff'd
  My unpolluted truth—
Oh, it was death to feel the venom-dews
  Trickling the veins of youth!

My mind was swung in blindness, like a cloud,
  O'er caverns of despair;
My soul was a dead Carthage, with a doomed
  And baffled Roman there.

Stung by the blare and trespass of the world,
  I cursed it, on my knees,
Where, in its cell, monastic Amazon
  Hymns to the cloistered trees.

## PALINODIA

I wrestled with my soul when twilight fowls
  Began their rigadoon,
Where the lost cypress, like Ophelia, mourns
  Above the gaunt lagoon.

Dumb with disaster, we did grapple on,
  Like Ghibbeline and Guelph;
Though I could flee all other things beside,
  I could not flee—myself.

Yes! I have pillaged the forbidden boughs
  Of all their stealthy lore;
The fruit that shed its dust upon my lips
  Was from Gomorrha's shore.

Love! I will cleanse those lips at Siloe's pool,
  Incumbent to the sod;
I look upon my Past, as Pagan's look
  Upon their cloven god.

Love ! will kneel at holier knees again,
  With sin-abashing brow,
And learn a new Philosophy from Faith
  To save me from the slough.

Love! it was thy meek eyes and gentle words
  That gave my spirit sight,
And it will follow thee to higher laws
  Through the dim Vale of Night.

---

## MALISON

I promised no reproach, Elise,
Though all thy flimsy vows were fickle;
My slender-necked anemones
Have perished by thy crafty sickle;
Well! let them go, though soiled and stolen,
And headless, too, as Anna Boleyn—
Ay, let them go, though debonnair
With hazel, poppy-perfumed hair.
I'll not reproach, Elise, but I
Will make my malediction lie
Upon thee, feathery as a sigh;
Till from abysmal peaks of woe
My curse shall shroud thee with its snow;

## MALISON

Softly upon the forehead fair,
Crisping the poppy-perfumed hair,
Its winnowing ice-birds lilt and go,—
But no reproach, Elise, oh no—
Only the rustle of the snow!
'Twill skim thy throat not rude or redly—
    Its dapper feet,
    Slippered with sleet,
Shall into thy bonnet and bossom retreat
    With a stinging like snow,
    Which is woe—
Only my curse, my curse you know!
    Not rude or redly—
    Nothing but snow!
As shy—as smooth—as cool—as slow—
    As deadly.

## CLAY

Written on the occasion of the unveiling of the Clay Statue, April 12th, 1860

Immortal Mind! thy burning torch
  A deathless halo flings
Around the Prophets crucified,
  And Sybaritic Kings;
We chaunt, today, a pæan song
  To thy divinest flashes—
To our imperishable one,
  The Mill Boy of the Slashes!

The fervid breast of Nature poured
  Its deluge to his sips,
The bee-winged breezes charmed anew
  Hymettus to his lips,
Till, like a cleaving peak, his thoughts
  To sunward regions ran,
And god beheld beneath his throne
  A mountain hearted *Man.*

## CLAY

His lispings fell like vesper dews
  Upon the alien leaves,
Waking their inspirations through
  The palpitating sheaves;
Then from those clarion "wood-notes wild"
  Anointed dreams unsprung,
Wedding the lightning of the brain
  To the thunder of the tongue!

We—we have seen him in the pride
  Of his colossal youth,
We—we have heard his Vestal vows
  To the Eternal Truth;
We—we have felt our spirits quail,
  Our very beings bow,
When the supernal tempests shook
  That monumental brow!

And never yet, since morning stars
  Sang over Galilee,
Have nations seen the peer of this
  Apostle of the free!
His was the avalanche of wrath
  That smites the despot down,
And girds the brows of Justice with
  An undisheveled crown.

His trumpet-tones re-echoed like
  Evangels to the free,
Where Chimborazo views a world
  Mosaic'd in the sea;
And his proud form shall stand erect
  In that triumphal car
Which bears to the Valhalla gates
  Heroic Bolivar!

He spoke for Greece, and freedom flew
  Along her sacred rills,
Waking the mighty soul that slept
  On Marathinian hills;
While bold Buzzards launched his flag
  Upon the gull of night,
And hurled a living thunderbolt
  Against the Ottomite!

The pillars of the Union quaked
  Before discordant shocks,
When Heaven had sent its liberal snows
  Upon his honored locks;
Though all the Angels beckoned him,
  His conquering arm uprose,
And wrenched his country's flag away
  From its rebellious foes.

CLAY

Then with perennial laurel wreaths,
The matchless mind had wrought,
His ladened bark went drifting on
To find the "Kings of Thought;"
And though the stately vessel long
Hath left its earthly strand,
The helmsman's voice re-echoes back
From out the Phantom Land.

Live, Patriot, live! while oceans chafe
Their adamantine bars—
While mailed Orion flames his plume
'Mid bright-battalioned stars;
Live, Patriot, live! while glory thrills
The heart-strings of the free,
And Mississippi pours its grand
Libations to the sea!

## THE UNBOUGHT SEMINOLE

After the defection of many of the Seminole chiefs in 1857, Arpeik was approached by the United States Commissioners, and tendered money and lands if he would cease hostilities and consent to deportation. Though not less than one hundred and fourteen years old, blind and decrepit, his intellect survived the wreck of the body and his soul retained its ancient heat. His reply was worthy of any age: "Wagon loads of gold shall never buy me!" A few months afterward, he died and was buried among the Thousand Islands in a remote corner of the land which gave him birth, which he had fought to possess and which he never relinguished utterly.

An old, old man, in thicker shades
  Than brood upon the brows of Night,
Hath lit the ghastly Everglades
  With an imperishable light;
A light more brilliant in its flame
  From the dusk soul from whence it came,
Amid the war-cloud's clashing fame—

## THE UNBOUGHT SEMINOLE

It burns! it blazes! let it be
A globe-mark for the bold and free
To beacon on Eternity.
Ay, let it flash its halo high—
Flash like a meteor in the sky
With lightning flame
To carve a name
That cannot, will not quickly die!

No subtle tribute of the mine
Could quell that hero-heart of thine;
Not the ripe wilderness of gold
Through which Pactolian tides have roll'd;
Not the star-gem that grandly flings
Its flambeau by barbaric kings;
No traitor's breath, no hostile band,
Not Power's all-pervading hand
Could wrench thee from thy native land.
The lone wolf from his lair
May find a shelter from despair—
Man of the weary-foot, for thee
No refuge held the land or sea—
Death, death alone could set thee free—
And, more than free, since thus it came
Girt with the glory-wings of fame.

O, wildwood Spartan of thy time!
O more than Roman in thy crime,
Love for thine own beloved clime.
Dear God! what segment of the earth
Can match the region of our birth!
Though ice-beleagured, rill on rill,
Though scorched to deserts, hill on hill—
It is our native country still.
Our native country, what a sound
To make heart, brain, and blood rebound!
Our native country! bannered far
On eagle wings, with cross and star;
Diviner than the hymns of glee
That flood Astarte-eyed Chaldee,
It frets the war flag on the deep,
It makes the bale-fire on the steep,
It stirs a thought that cannot sleep.

It arsenals the fleetest arm
With the keen weapons of alarm,
And sends them shimmering forth amain
To smite and smite and smite again.
It boomed a grand, cathedral bell
Along the crags to Bruce and Tell;
It rang like cymbals on the breeze
To Henry and Demosthenes;

THE UNBOUGHT SEMINOLE

It pealed, like trumpets in the fray
  That canonized Thermopylae;
It wailed o'er Warren, sad and shrill,
  In the hot crash of Bunker Hill;
It wept wild music o'er the dart
  That burst from Osceola's heart,
And still fares forth, a choral wave
  Upon the never-dying brave.
Such, such the heavenly-gardened seed
  That flowers each immortal deed.

Such, such the spirit of the past
  That nobly battles to the last,
And such the sunbeam of thy soul,
  Grim Brutus of the Seminole!
And I—though pale-faced and thy foe,
  Can laud thy joy and feel thy woe;
Would that a Homer's magic lyre,
  His Sybil lip, his tongue of fire,
Were mine but one great moment—then,
  Statued with monumental men,
Thy ghostly form, rapt in renown,
  Should stand with helmet, sword, and crown—
  And who would dare to drag it down?

* * * * * * * * *

From the throned summit of the Thousand Islands
  Meek virgins of the sea;
Along their diadem of emerald highlands,
  The death-song sobs for thee.

The gay magnolia musky-haired and tender,
  Queen-dryad of the scene,
Snares, in its veil of flower-floating splendor,
  Winged linguist of the green.

The bright-plumed cedar trails its daintiest pillow
  For nectar-laden bees;
Kneels, by the lake, the tress-disheveled willow,
  Lone Magdalen of trees!

The knightly oak, a bulwark swart and brawny,
  Stands by its page the vine;
Or hangs its large, storm-gullied, cleft, and tawny,
  Upon its spear, the pine.

A dreamy fleck of violet creations
  Stare at the anchored clouds,
Or shrink to see the spectral cypress nations
  Rise glittering through their shrouds.

## THE UNBOUGHT SEMINOLE

Beneath the turban of a tall palmetto,
  Thy scattered warriors kneel,
Grim pilgrims at their gallant heart's Loretto,
  With votive bead and steel.

Upon their hearts, broad bucklers of alliance,
  The scars are greenly dim'd—
Dread gaps, dread syllables of fierce defiance
  Upon the tiger-limbed.

Apart from all, of all the goodliest number
  Are widowed ones, alas!
In vain, in vain ye watch for those who slumber
  In lagoon and morass.

A giant mound, with untold ages hoary
  Outspiraling the strand,
Bears thee, great chieftain, like a steed of glory,,
  Upon the spirit-land.

From the grey summit of Time's stateliest mountain,
  Age, throned amid the rocks,
Had shot the avalanche of a thousand fountains
  In silver down thy locks.

But now, but now, thy earthliness departed,
De Leon's fount is won;
And all the dead who left thee, broken hearted,
Outgleam the primal sun.

There Micanopy, with his plumes vermilion,
Stalks by the glittering ring,
There Tustenuggee, 'neath a rich pavilion,
Ay "every inch a King!"

There Osceola, warlike, wise and sparing,
Outsoars the belting wave,
There Coacbochee, warlike, wild and daring,
From his bleak western grave.

There, the Great Spirit, in his car of thunder,
Salutes thee with a smile,
"Live on, my son!" The clouds are rent asunder
About the funeral pile.

Dark Withlacoochee caught the magic meaning,
Triumphant with St. John,
And bore it on, with every ripple gleaming,
"Live on! Live on! Live on!"

## AFTER A LITTLE WHILE

The comeliest damsels of thy shadowy nation
  Shall sing to thee: "Live on!"
Shout echo, million-tongued o'er the nation,
  "Live on! Live on! Live on!"

The lyric gales, in soft melodious motion,
  Thrill the harp-pines: "Live on!"
While throbs the everlasting dirge of ocean:
  "Live on! Live on! Live on!"

---

## AFTER A LITTLE WHILE

After a little while,
When all the glories of the night and day
Have fled for aye,
From Friendship's glance and Beauty's win-
some smile,
I pass away,
After a little while.

After a little while,
The snow will fall from time and trial shocks
Down these dark locks;
Then gliding onward to the Golden Isle,
I pass the rocks,
After a little while.

After a little while,
Perchance, when youth is blazoned on my brow,
As Hope is now,
I fade and quiver in this dim defile,
A fruitless bough,
After a little while.

After a little while,
And clouds that shimmer on the robes of June
And vestal moon,
No more my vagrant fancies can beguile—
I slumber soon,
After a little while.

After a little while,
The birds will serenade in bush and tree,
But not for me;
On billows duskier than the gloomy Nile
My barque must be—
After a little while.

## THE PLACE OF REST

After a little while,
The cross will glisten and the thistles wave
Above my grave,
And planets smile;
Sweet Lord! then pillowed on Thy gentle breast,
I fain would rest,
After a little while.

---

## THE PLACE OF REST

I am not happy, though my smiles betoken
The jocund fancies which I do not feel;
I am not happy, all my hopes are broken
Upon the world's inexorable wheel.
'Tis said the dying shed no useless tears,
And so, I weep not for the vanished years.

I weep not for them, though they flock around me
In solitude, and in the noontide glare;
I weep not for them, though fond eyes confound me,
With midnight havened in their realmless stare.
With jests upon my lips I stand aghast
O'er the Dead Angel that we call the Past.

No More! O terrible, wild word! the days
  That have been shudder in the iron grave;
And lo, I totter on, in blind amaze,
  'Mid the black gulches of th' o'erwhelming wave:
No star-bright seas, no Pharos-litten shore,
  While the hoarse Raven croaks, "No More! No More!"

And still I weep not, it may be, alas!
  That I am hardened into more than stone—
Ah, happy they whose hearts like brittle glass,
  Break ere the worst of bitterness is known.
The cold remain, the gentle pass away,
  In their white innocence—how happy they!

The drums are clattering in the crowded streets,
  The fife and bugle warlike concords blend,
The roar of cannon to my soul repeats:
  Peace, weary one, thy pilgrimage can end—
There's rest for thee upon the battle field,
  With Triumph towering in thy shattered shields!

## "REFUGE OF SINNERS"

Though loathsome sin, usurping grace,
Should make my soul its dwelling place;
Though Satan, with his host of flame,
Combined to crush my spirit's fame;
I'd look to heav'n—avaunt despair!
Because I have a Mother there.

Though man should couch foul slander's dart
To pierce with death my wounded heart;
Though trusted friends, nay, all that's dear
Should flee my sight—without a tear,
I'd waft on high an earnest prayer,
Because I have a Mother there.

Though the poor beggar's staff be mine,
And all despise, I'll not repine;
Though hunger writes upon my cheek
Its fatal mark, in Winter's bleak;
For heaven's sake all this I'll bear,
Because I have a Mother there.

Though God should call to Him above,
Snatching away mine early love;
An earthly mother wrap away
From hence to realms of endless day;
I would not bid our dear Lord spare,
Because I'd have two Mothers there.

When I am with the countless dead,
When wild weeds riot o'er my head,
One boon I ask, one favor crave:
Let one true mourner guard my grave,
And let my soul seek regions fair,
Because it has a Mother there.

# MOTHER AND SON

## MOTHER AND SON

Thirty years ago two of my Catholic friends, fond parents, were called upon to endure a grievous tribulation in the death, by accidental drowning, of a noble virtuous son. I promised the father to write a poem on this sad theme, but, somehow, in the distraction of active secular journalism and the need of practical support for a growing family, I could not accomplish that purpose. A few days ago, with more leisure and a return of the long-neglected gift. I determined to pay the debt, and as some hearts may be comforted by sympathetic verse, I take the liberty of asking The Columbian to reproduce the poem, for the first time:

'Tis thirty years, my son,<br>
  Since we were parted;<br>
Thy bright course swiftly run—<br>
  I, broken hearted,<br>
Hast thou been gone so long<br>
  To realms of light,<br>
To choirs of angel-song,<br>
  To visions bright?

When thou wert rapt away
By the stern tide,
I taught thee how to pray—
In innocence abide.
So, though thy call was brief,
With no good-bye,
I know, with firm belief,
'Twas well to die.

Thy piety and worth
Were all secure;
Yea, from thy Christian birth
Thy days were pure.
And so, the God of love
Claimed thee His own.
Thy spirit winged above
To seek its throne.

Father and mother both
Gave thee to bliss;
Resigned, however loath,
Thy parting kiss.
We learned to bless the hour
Thy soul should be
Beyond all sinful power
And grandly free.

## MOTHER AND SON

Thy father saw thee first
  In Christ's abode;
His spirit was athirst
  For Heaven's road.
Thy mother will await
  The last decree
That opens glory's gate
  To welcome thee.

To meet and see again
  Thy sire and thee,
Beyond the reach of pain,
  In ecstacy.
This is thy mother's prayer,
  And this her goal.
To love and bless thee there,
  Soul unto soul.

## THE ONLY BOY

Though heaven has gained one angel more,
My heart, dear God, is wondrous sore;
For that bright angel Thou hast won
Was my sweet lamb, my only son.

How shall an earthly mother bear
Such awful anguish and despair?
How shall she live, and living, know
Such depths of overwhelming woe?

Without Thy aid, dear God, my soul
Is shipwrecked in a sea of dole.
Without Thy rescuing hand, I sink
Beyond the world's absymal brink.

He was my pride, my hope, my joy—
Ah, bitterest thought, *my only boy!*
And now, while night-winds madly rave
My heart is buried in his grave.

## THE ONLY BOY

Too much I worshiped him, perchance
Too much I drifted from Thy glance.
Thou art a jealous God, and Thou
Hast put Thy crown upon my brow.

I pass beneath Thy rod; I pray
To find salvation's thorny way—
I care not boy what pangs beguiled,
So it but lead me to my child.

Ah, blessed thought to know that he
Is safe from sin and misery;
That, in the young May of his life,
He fell unsullied in the strife.

I treasure up his image fair,
I kiss his tress of shining hair,
Thrilling to hope, in heaven, that he
Will be "the first to welcome me."

Within Thy sheltering arms, I place
My idol, glorified by grace;
And, with the dear ones left, my eyes
Gaze through the gates of Paradise.

## LABOR AND PRAYER

Despite the wisdom of the Past,
  From lips prophetic or divine,
Men wander in this world aghast,
  And ask another saving sign.
They seek cold Science in her cell,
  With front of brass and feet of clay;
And this is what her sibyls tell:
  "The man who labors need not pray!"

Starving upon this soulless rind,
  The pilgrim, weary with his strife,
Cries to the proud poetic mind:
  "Sing to us, seer, the psalm of life!"
The bard, with sensual lore endowed,
  Unclasps his dreamy Book of Fate,
And answers: "Let the famished crowd
  First learn to labor and to wait!"

## LABOR AND PRAYER

With spirit-hunger humbler grown,
  The seeker lifts his saddened eyes
To Him whose everlasting throne
  Fills all the earth and all the skies;
And from that oracle of might,
  Healing the torment of the rod,
List to the accents of delight:
  "The germ of action glows in God!"

The sum of all is: Seek ye first
  The heavenly kingdom Christ restored,
Exclaiming, with supernal thirst,
  "The glory Thine alone, O Lord!"
Then shall descend celestial rest,
  Unknown to children of despair,
The consecration of the Blest,
  In labor, patience, faith and prayer!

Labor, to do the best we may,
  In patient kinship with our trust;
Faith, to illume the coming day
  That wakes the tragic trance of dust;
Prayer, to deserve the Guiding Hand,
  Without whose grasp our steps are vain—
Lord! to thy other Living Land
  Link us with that electric chain!

## IN MEMORIAM

Father and Lord! We know full well
  Thy chastisements are for the best;
  And while the loved and lost are blest,
Our hearts throb like a funeral bell,
  Although the weary are at rest.

We bow to Thy decree, we bow
  To that dread stroke which bore away,
  To regions of eternal day,
Our darling boy, whose starry brow
  Beamed like a golden morn of May.

And yet, dear God, how hard to yield,
  Even to Thee, that precious life—
  Bequeathed to glory without strife,
Without a scar or battle-field—
  But with Love's tenderest virtues rife.

He came to us as sunshine falls
  Upon a sorrow-stricken hearth.
  He came with innocence and mirth;
His voice made music in our halls—
  How can we hide him in the earth?

## IN MEMORIAM

Thou who wast scourged and crucified
  For fallen man! behold to-night
  A mother smitten in Thy sight.
Behold how all her hopes have died!
  Send her Thy comfort and Thy light!

Tell her that when the cruel wave
  Closed o'er her child's benignant head,
  The Lord of Life in mercy sped,
To glorify him in the grave
  And raise an angel from the dead.

Too pure to combat this dark globe,
  Too gentle for the madding crowd,
  Better thy unpolluted shroud,
Thy early death, thy spotless robe,
  Than many years with sadness bowed.

Ah! we who loved thee so will keep
  Thy memory a sacred trust,
  A sweet evangel from the dust,
To cheer us when we wail and weep,
  While thou art dwelling with the Just!

Dedicated to MRS. ALBERT BALDWIN

## CUTHBERT IN HEAVEN

Beautiful mother
Of a beautiful boy,
Life is Death's brother.
Weep not for him
Who from the world dim
Rose to the realm of perpetual joy.

Thank God for giving,
Thank Him for taking.
To the Land of the Living
Cuthbert has flown,
By the White Throne,
Where the earth-sleepers in Heaven are waking.

## CUTHBERT IN HEAVEN

No mortal bliss
Can match his above—
You've an angel to kiss,
When you aspire
To the home of desire,
Filled with an infinite Mercy and Love.

Always to you
He will be glorious,
"Tender and true."
Out of great sorrow
Comes a bright morrow,
When your strong soul will meet him victorious.

He went before
To lead you aright—
To endure and adore:
Free from all stain,
You shall meet him again,
Crowned and caressed in kingdoms of light.

Better by far
To know he is blest,
Like a radiant star,
Than bruised by the blow
Of the world in its woe—
Better God's wonderful, mystical rest.

Happy is he,
Made a present to God,
That his mother might see
    Her way to the skies.
    By the path of the wise,
Where the chosen who triumph in anguish have trod.

Christ, in His passion,
Teaches your heart
How sadness may fashion,
    With wonderful grace,
    The soul for its place
Where mothers and children have never to part.

Cling to the Cross
    That was sent you to save
From terrible loss,
    Till you have risen
    From the tomb's prison,
Welcomed by Christ who has conquered the grave!

SUNDAY REVERY

## SUNDAY REVERY

Beyond my dingy window pane,
  This beamy Sunday morn,
I watch the red-breast on the vane
  And the ravens robbing corn;
Hard by, the Alabama boils
  Its sallow flood along,
With drift-wood biers and forest spoils—
  A melancholy throng!

The rich horizon melts away
  To an illumined arch,
With summer tresses all astray
  Upon the brows of March;
The birds, inebriate with glees,
  Seem happiest when they sing,
Thrilling the aromatic trees
  With symphonies of Spring.

The pulse of nature throbs anew
  Impassioned of the sun;
The violet, with eyes of blue,
  Is modest as a nun.
The roses reck not of the strife
  That crashes up the North;
Alas! the mockery of life
  When Death is striding forth.

An alien in this lonely land,
  I sound an alien strain,
Until my own fair State shall stand
  Inviolate again;
The long-lost Pleiad of our sky
  Is glimmering still afar,
And nations yet shall see on high
  That bright and blessed star.

The church bells toll their solemn chime,
  From out the minster eaves,
Knelling some old religious rhyme,
  Half stifled by the leaves.
A thousand miles away, I hear
  Those grand Cathedral notes,
Which made my youth a fairy sphere
  With cymbal-clashing throats.

## SUNDAY REVERY

Vibrating to each sturdy tone,
  My soul remembers well
The mild Madonna's statue-stone
  Within its ivory cell;
The ritual read, the chanting done—
  The belfry music roll'd,
And all my faith, like Whittington,
  Was in the tales it told!

And, oh! I feel as men must feel
  Who have not wept for years;
Upon my cheek behold the seal
  Of consecrated tears.
A mighty Sabbath calm is mine
  That baffles human lore,
A resurrection of Lang Syne
  A guiltless child once more.

And mother's school-boy with his mimes,
  This beamy Sunday morn,
Forgets the grim, tumultuous times
  That hardened him in scorn.
Forgets terrific ocean days
  Beyond the tropic gates,
Where the Magellan clouds down-gaze
  On Patagonian Straits.

He nothing heeds the long despair
  Within the savage swamp,
The jungle and the thicket where
  The serpent tribes encamp;
He little heeds the dream of Fame,
  Its treason or its trust,
The hope of a sonorous name—
  A requiem from the dust.

But oh, he heeds Elysian hours
  That hint of Long Ago!
Those dreamful days in college towers
  He never more shall know—
The home he never more may see,
  A Paradise to him—
The books he read at Mother's knee
  When her dear eyes grew dim!

O Mother—Mother! Tears must fleet
  Along the battle track
Ere yet thy lonely heart can greet
  Its weary wanderer back—
A deathless love these tears bespeak,
  For thy devotion shed,
With thy pure kisses on my cheek,
  Thy blessing on my head!

## LA FETE DES MORTS

## LA FETE DES MORTS

Peace to the dead; though the skies are chill,
And the Norse wind waileth coarse and shrill.
Peace to the dead! though the living shake
The globe, with their brawling battle-quake.
Peace to the dead! though peace is not
In the regal dome or the pauper cot.
Peace to the dead; there's peace, we trust,
With the pale dreamers in the dust.

Roses and pansies guard them well,
Tinging triumphant immortelle,
Minions of Doubt, we bend the knee
To the kings and queens of mystery.
Storm and sunshine, mist and rain,
Do ye mock at their marble doors in vain?
And ye, sepulchral cliffs of night,
Do ye rise to appeal their shadowed sight?
O Darkness! thy mission is not just
To the pale dreamers in the dust.

Peace to the dead! afar and near,
In folds of satin or beggar's bier,
Whether they sleep in the kirk-yard ground,
Or bleach in the gullied seas profound;
Garnered by Time's dull scimitar,
Or cleft in the scarlet fields of war;
Godless is he who breaketh the crust
Of the Past, o'er the dreamers in the dust.

Peace to the mother, there beguiled
With her frozen lily—her deathless child;
Peace to the father and his mate,
Peace to the lowly and the great,
Peace to the maidens as they rest
With the cross on the cold and waxen breast;
Peace to the soldier, blossom and bud,
For he fell with the sacrament of blood;
Peace to the dead! there's peace, we trust,
With the pale dreamers in the dust.

Father! if peace is not with them,
Where shall we seek for the subtle gem?
'Tis not of the Earth, for we lose it here,
And death is the gate of the golden sphere.
Father! Thy mercies cannot cease;
Crush us, but give Thy sleepers peace.
Smite us, Redeemer, if Thou must,
But pardon the dreamers in the dust!

*New Orleans, Nov.* 2, 1862.

# NIGHT AND DAY

## NIGHT AND DAY

Night above and night below—
Into the night you saw me go,
With the midnight of my woe.

Had I never sought your side,
You had never stung my pride;
Then my faith had never died.

I was made to think you dear—
Madder far to kiss the spear—
Maddest, that I lingered here.

Welcome back, good pilgrim's staff!
Truth is wind, and Love is chaff—
Both are winnowed by a laugh.

Hola ho; I will depart
Though seditious tear-drops start—
Though each foot-fall stabs my heart!

Sink or swim I'll tempt the stream;
In your eye's repellant beam
Tombing what I dared to dream.

Day above and day below—
Into the day you'll see me go,
With the day-break stars—heigho.

## LOST AND SAVED

When thou wert born into the world,
  My darling little child,
A robin came a second time
  And piped its "wood-notes wild."
When thou wert laid away to rest,
  Beneath the churchyard clay,
A robin came a second time
  To sing a mournful lay.

Did the bird come to solace me
  With message from the skies,
When thou wert welcomed to the earth
  And then to Paradise?
Was it thy guardian spirit, love,
  That met me, first and last,
Across the sparkling bridge that spans
  The Future and the Past?

## LOST AND SAVED

Dear robin, with the tender heart,
  I know how it is said
Your snowy bosom once became
  A holy tint of red.
'Twas on the Saviour's thorny crown
  You bruised your dainty breast,
And unto you and Him I come
  For comfort and for rest.

Lord! thou hast given me a child
  And taken her away!
Behold me prostrate in the dust,
  A mourner night and day.
My heart is empty and my soul
  Rebellious in Thy sight—
Grant me the boon of perfect trust,
  And lead me to the light.

Teach me that it was surely best
  My one ewe lamb should go
Beyond the starry gems of night
  And wilderness of woe.
Teach me that on some radiant shore,
  Beyond th' eternal main,
I shall behold her glorious eyes,
  And clasp her form again!

Lord! I am in the Vale of Death!
  No beacon burns within;
Send me a vision of my child
  To break the spell of sin.
Bid her come as a bird and say:
  "Mother, look up and see
How I am saved for endless joy—
  Sweet mother! follow me!

"Had I remained upon the earth,
  As you so fiercely prayed,
There would have come a dismal fate
  To grieve your little maid.
Sorrow and sickness and despair
  Would toss my soul about,
Till I should live a life of pain
  And die the death of doubt.

"Christ, in His mercy and His love,
  Has spared your darling this,
Giving instead a home divine
  And everlasting bliss.
Lo! He has bid me fly to you,
  And in the twilight dim,
Reveal how I was called away
  To lead you on to Him!

## LOST AND SAVED

"Mother! the faith that guides to God
  Will bring your soul to me;
There is no other certain way
  Your cherub child to see.
Close not your ears to this appeal
  That calms all human strife,
Making the gloomy grave itself
  The Golden Gate of Life!

"The love that shall not lose its own
  Must seek celestial fire—
Must light its torch by Heavenly flame,
  And not the Pagan pyre.
Mother! dear mother! hear your child,
  And let her win you where
The King of Glory sits enthroned
  With 'angels bright and fair.'

"And when the hour shall come for you
  To bid the world farewell,
I shall be hovering o'er your couch
  To hear the dying knell;
And you shall see me, robed in white,
  With the red-breast in my hand,
Thrilling to guide you gently on
  To the Eternal Land!"

My child! I hear thy voice and heed—
  I go to God and thee!
Lead thou me on to thy abode
  Beyond the sapphire sea!
And while thy little body sleeps
  Among the birds and flowers,
I know thy sinless spirit soars,
  In happier skies than ours!

# RESURGAM

## RESURGAM

Teach me, my God, to bear my cross,
  As thine was borne;
Teach me to make of every loss
  A crown of thorn.
Give me Thy patience and Thy strength
  With every breath,
Until my lingering days at length
  Shall welcome death.

Dear Jesus, I believe that Thou
  Did'st rise again,
Instill the spirit in me now
  That conquers pain.
Give me the grace to cast aside
  All vain desire,
All the fierce throbbing of a pride
  That flames like fire.

Give me the calm that Dante wrought
  From sensual din;
The peace that errant Woolsey sought
  From stalwart sin.
I seek repose upon Thy breast
  With child-like prayer;
Oh let me find the heavenly rest
  And mercy there!

If I have, in rebellious ways,
  Profaned my life;
If I have filled my daring days
  With worldly strife;
If I have shunned the narrow path
  In crime to fall—
Lead me from th' abode of wrath
  And pardon all!

Banished from Thee! where shall I find
  For my poor soul
A safe retreat from storms that blind,
  Or seas that roll?
Come to me, Christ, ere I, forlorn,
  Sink 'neath the wave,
And on this blessed Easter morn
  A lost one save!

www.ingramcontent.com/pod-product-compliance
Lightning Source LLC
LaVergne TN
LVHW011231110826
845150LV00006B/1606

* 9 7 8 1 4 2 5 5 1 4 5 2 5 *